EPHESIANS

A STUDY MANUAL

R. D. STUART

Presbyterian and Reformed Publishing Company
Phillipsburg, New Jersey

Scripture quotations are from the New American Standard Bible, Study Edition, A. J. Holman Company.

Manufactured in the United States of America

Library of Congress Cataloging-in-Publication Data

Stuart, R. D., 1945-
    Ephesians : a study manual.

    1. Bible. N.T. Ephesians—Study. I. Title.
BS2695.5.S78   1987   227'.506   86-30235
ISBN 0–87552–447–8 (pbk.)

Contents

Preface

This study is designed to be readily used and understood by men and women in our current age of busy schedules. The questions proposed in this inductive study can be answered without a major time investment on the part of the reader. Some questions are more difficult than others, and there is room for motivated students to dig deeper if they should desire.

First used in an adult Sunday school class the course had a sevenfold purpose: (1) to study the Word of God; (2) to apply the Word to our lives; (3) to learn how to reach out to others; (4) to learn how to disciple each other; (5) to begin recognizing needs of others; (6) to learn how to pray for and satisfy those needs; and (7) to learn how to receive help from others.

We supplied a notebook with five sections, entitled Commentary, Questions, Notes, Prayers, and Application. Although anyone could join the class at any time, we found that the course worked best with no more than ten people in a group, eight being the ideal number. A group leader had the following responsibilities: (1) to keep the discussions moving and to lead others to contribute to the discussions; (2) to keep people on the topic; (3) to send materials to those absent; (4) to encourage people to phone each other during the week (occasionally assigning people to do it); (5) to encourage the group to meet for lunch or dinner during the course of the study; and (6) to disciple one person whom the Lord laid on his heart.

The course was designed for a thirteen-week Sunday school quarter and could serve well in a home Bible study setting. Each session began with a time devoted to needs for prayer. The leader asked for specific prayer requests from the whole class, and people jotted down the requests in the prayer section of their notebooks. The following week the leader asked if anyone wished to share an answer to prayer, and the class recorded the date on which the Lord answered the prayer. Group members were encouraged to keep their notebooks near where they usually prayed at home and to pray throughout the week between studies. During the week they were also encouraged to write down other prayer concerns.

Next, the class discussed the questions proposed the previous week. This gave the teacher an idea of which questions were most interesting and challenging to the group members and of how to focus his teaching for that week. It also enabled him to get to know his students better. Students were encouraged to base their answers on the Scripture readings and not to depend on the commentary.

Then as the teacher covered the Scripture assigned, he concentrated on answering the questions that had been discussed.

The remaining time was given to application of the Scripture lesson, in which the teacher offered suggestions and asked members of the class to share how they might apply the Scripture to their lives. People were to check *yes* if they applied the previous lesson and *no* if they did not. Throughout the course, the class was encouraged to look back over the weeks and attempt to apply what they promised and failed to do. The application section of the notebook served as a spiritual barometer for students to see how often they applied Scripture to their daily lives.

The success of any study like this depends on the student's commitment to serve and follow the Lord Jesus. In our experience the study has proved rewarding as God has used it to enable us to grow. May it prove beneficial to many others as well.

1

Introduction and Background

Authorship

The Letter to the Ephesians proclaims its authorship in the first verse: "Paul, an apostle of Christ Jesus by the will of God." Again, at the beginning of the third chapter, the writer identifies himself: "For this reason I, Paul . . ." Though ancient scholars never contested Paul's authorship, modern critics (from 1820 to the present) have done just that. These critics claim that the Letter to the Ephesians has a distinctive style and vocabulary from Paul's other letters. Not only is this a subjective argument, but it fails to credit Paul with ingenuity and creativity. These critics would rather paint Paul as a very staid and inflexible writer than give him literary credit for using different words. The circumstances that prompt a letter lead the author in developing and stressing one or more themes. Varied themes normally necessitate new and different words. Furthermore, if Paul had another person writing for him, such as Tychicus (6:21), the style would be different, yet the thoughts would still be Paul's.

Critics base another argument against Paul's authorship on what they believe is a discrepancy with the Book of Acts. Acts 19:1–20:1 records that Paul on his second visit stayed with the Ephesians for three years. During this time the Ephesians came to know him in such an intimate manner that, when Paul finally left, they were saddened to tears and moved to hug and kiss him (Acts 20:37). The critics exploit this bit of emotion by claiming that Paul would have had personal greetings to his beloved Ephesians. In other words, the letter should have personally mentioned his friends as did his Letter to the Romans.

The letter does have an impersonal tone, probably because Paul was not directly addressing the believers at Ephesus. He wrote to all the churches in the province of Asia; the letter was not limited to one church. Rather, Paul intended that the letter be distributed among other churches in the province of which Ephesus was the most known. The Letter to the Colossians verifies this view: Colossians 4:7 says Tychicus will bring additional information to the Colossians; Ephesians 6:21 mentions that Tychicus will make everything known to them. Tychicus was the messenger who carried both letters, which were written at approximately the same time to a destination in the same general area. But don't the words "to the saints at Ephesus" establish once and for all that the letter was directed to the Ephesians? Not really, for two of the earliest and most authoritative manuscripts do not contain the words "at Ephesus."

A third argument against Paul's authorship is theological. Unlike other Pauline letters, Ephesians speaks about the heavenly sphere where the powers and principalities operate and not about justification and dying with Christ. The emphasis, say the critics, concerns both the church and reconciliation between Jew and Gentile, rather than between God and sinners. In an effort to be intellectual, the critics have become as "yellow journalists" and focused on minor variations without seeing the major evidence for Pauline theology. The doctrines of election (1:4), of adoption (1:5), of grace (2:4), of Christian unity (4:4), and of family relationships (5:22–6:9) are all present in this letter as well as letters of uncontested Pauline authorship.

Paul is clearly the author of Ephesians. To state otherwise is to say that the Letter to the Ephesians perpetrates a fraud, for the letter itself presents Paul as the author. For anyone to study a book of the Bible that he or she believes was not written by the person it specifies as its author is an effort in obscurantism. For if the book perpetrates fraud, it does not deserve to be studied. If one part of the letter is false, then no part of the letter can be trusted. Those who study the letter believing it to be a fraud are fools who despise wisdom and instruction (Prov. 1:7). In thinking they are wise with new theories and criticisms, they have become fools (Rom. 1:22) who not only stumble over their own folly, but also lead others astray to their own detriment.

Time and Place of Writing

The letter indicates that Paul was a prisoner at the time of its composition. Paul mentions that he was a "prisoner of Christ Jesus for the sake of you Gentiles" (3:1), a "prisoner of the Lord" (4:1), and an "ambassador in chains" (6:20). The Book of Acts speaks about two lengthy periods of Paul's imprisonment. One was in Caesarea (Acts 24:27), and the other was in Rome (Acts 28:30). Both lasted two years, which would have allowed Paul sufficient time to receive information about believers in various churches and correspond with them. Because of the orderly progression of Paul's thought throughout his ministry (mainly systematic and doctrinal), the most likely dating of the letter is during his Roman imprisonment, some-time between A.D. 60 and 63. The Letter to the Ephesians was written at about the same time as Philemon and Colossians and, most likely, immediately after Colossians. Both letters appear to have been sent by way of Tychicus, who visited Paul.

Recipients

Since there is a connection with the Letter to the Colossians, the destination of both must have been in the same general area. Colossae and Ephesus are in the province of Asia. As discussed under the section on authorship, the recipients included not just Ephesians but all believers in the province. Hence, the letter lacks personal references. Paul never intended the message to be restricted to one church, but rather to be disseminated to others.

Reason for the Letter

The Letter to the Ephesians has close affinity with the Letter to the Colossians. In Colossae, there arose a form of false teaching that relegated Christ to a secondary position among the hierarchies of principalities and powers. In this scheme of the universe, Christ was not supreme, and His redemptive work was partial and incomplete. Paul wrote Colossians to combat this heresy.

Although the Colossian letter stressed the preeminence of Christ, it failed to envelop the theme of Christ's redemptive work in relation to the whole universe. The Colossians were told that God delivered them from darkness and transferred them into the kingdom of Christ (Col. 1:13). But what did it mean to be in Christ's kingdom? What did God expect of believers? And if the church is the body of the preeminent Christ, what is the believers' relation to Christ's cosmic role? Paul did not answer these questions in his letter to the Colossians.

Thus Paul penned another letter to these same people to instruct them further. As a community of believers they represented a new society created by God. This new society existed only because of the shed blood of Christ. God chose the church as a new community to be His earthly dwelling in which and from which His Holy Spirit would operate. The Letter to the Ephesians stresses that God works through those whom He has chosen by grace. Believers, individually and corporately, were created for the purpose of good works (2:10).

As a new community created in Christ Jesus, believers are made part of God's reconciling work in the universe. Although Paul mentions the theme of reconciliation in the Letter to the Colossians (Col. 1:20), he carries it further in the Letter to the Ephesians. If God's purpose is to sum up all things in Christ (1:10) and use His church in the process, the church must be the prime example of reconciliation—hence, the reconciliation of Jew and Gentile into one body (2:16). There is no better way to unveil a new society than by bonding together Jew and Gentile into one new entity (2:15). The world would take notice, for in Paul's time it was unheard of to have Jew and Gentile fellowshipping under the same banner. Only through Christ could this occur.

If the church is to be effective, men must see her conforming to the purposes and precepts of God. If she is to proclaim the gospel of reconciliation, nonbelievers must see a community of reconciled people. For this reason, Paul admonishes his readers and sets down practical requirements for living a life unified in Christ. The community of believers must illustrate in real life the new work done by God. The church accomplishes this by demonstrating unity, not divisiveness, in the body of Christ, as well as purity and love (4:1-3).

Questions for Ephesians 1:1-14

1. What do you think are the qualifications for being an apostle (1:1)?

2. What do you believe Paul meant when he said God "chose us in Him before the foundation of the world" (1:4)? How do you answer the critics who say this means we have no free choice?

   a.

   b.

3. Some people believe that everybody is a child of God. But God only had one Son! How, then, do we become children of God (1:5)?

   a. See Romans 8:14-17.

b. But what about Jesus' statement in John 10:34? Jesus quotes Psalm 82:6 in addressing the Pharisees. Does this mean that we are all children of God? Why not?

(1)

(2)

4. What does it mean to be sealed in Him (1:13)?

2

Christ's Redemptive Blessings

—————————————— *1:1-14* ——————————————

Who Is an Apostle?

The word "apostle" (1:1) comes from the Greek word *apostolos*. It is used some seventy-nine times in the New Testament. Eighty percent of these appear in the writings of Paul and his disciple Luke. *Apostolos* derives from the verb *apostellō*, which means "send forth." An apostle is one who is sent forth. In the New Testament, the term has an even more restrictive meaning, for an apostle was one sent forth bearing the message of the gospel. Does this indicate that there were more than the twelve, or thirteen if Matthias is included (Acts 1:26), apostles?

The term "apostle" first described the original disciples (eleven, excluding Judas) and then Paul. The term became a title that carried with it the authority of the One (Jesus Christ) sending forth those who carried the gospel message. Although godly men still preach the gospel message today, they cannot be considered apostles. Though they may and should have been called by God to preach, they do not fit the four requisites for apostleship. First, an apostle must have been an eyewitness to the resurrected Christ (I Cor. 9:1). Christ Himself appeared in bodily form to the eleven disciples who were chosen and called by Christ at the beginning of His ministry (Mark 16:14; Matt. 28:16-17). Christ also appeared to Paul on the road to Damascus (Acts 9:3-6).

What about today? Could not Christ appear to someone who could thereby claim apostleship? Although Christ could appear to whomever He might desire, we would have to ask, "For what reason?" Since the canon of Scripture is closed and revelation has been summed up in Christ Jesus, there can be no new revelation. If there were, then we would add to Scripture in direct violation of the Word itself. For God through Moses commanded us not to add to or take away from His Word or commandments (Deut. 4:2). Proverbs 30:5 tells us that every word of God is tested. We must not challenge His Word or add to it (Prov. 30:6), for a plague or other consequence may befall us (Rev. 22:18). So then, if a person claims Christ told him something new, we cannot accept it, for it would contradict Scripture.

Second, an apostle must have been discipled by Christ. The original eleven disciples walked, talked, and ate with Christ. They spent many hours under His personal teaching. They gave up at least three years of their lives to be with Him. At the Sermon on the Mount, Christ specifically directed His message to them: "And after He [Christ] sat down, His disciples came to Him, and opening His mouth, He began to teach them" (Matt. 5:1-2). Even Paul claimed to have been personally taught by Christ: "For I neither received it [the gospel] from man, nor was I taught it, but I received it through a revelation of Jesus Christ" (Gal. 1:12).

Third, an apostle must have been given authority by and been sent or commissioned by Christ. The eleven were given this authority in Matthew 28:18-20: "And Jesus came up and spoke to them saying, 'All authority has been given to Me in heaven and on earth. Go therefore and make diciples of all the nations, baptizing them in the name of the Father, and the Son and the Holy Spirit, teaching them all that I commanded you.'" Paul's commission is validated by Christ in Acts 26:16-18: "For this purpose I have appeared to you, to appoint you a minister and a witness not only to the things which you have seen, but also to the things in which I will appear to you."

Fourth, an apostle is recognized and validated by the other apostles. The eleven had no problem validating each other, for they were in Jesus' inner circle. They heard the words of Christ appointing them and commissioning them. They were at the Last Supper and heard Christ pray for them that they might be perfected in unity so that the world would know who Christ is (John 17:23). In that prayer Christ says He sent them into the world as His witnesses (John 17:18). They were also present together when Christ gave them the power to forgive sins (John 20:23). What about Paul? Was he recognized as an apostle by the others? Yes. When Paul presented himself before the council at Jerusalem, the apostles accepted him as God's choice to bring the gospel to the Gentiles (Acts 15:22-29). Peter also validated Paul's writing as equivalent to the rest of Scripture (II Pet. 3:16).

Did Matthias fit these criteria? We do not know if he saw the resurrected Christ, although he probably was one of the five hundred to whom Christ appeared (I Cor. 15:6). We do not know that he was personally discipled by Christ, although we do know that more than the twelve were discipled or taught by Jesus. In Luke 10:1, the Lord appointed and sent out seventy men preaching and healing. Although the first eleven recognized and validated Matthias as an apostle, Scripture gives no evidence that he was personally given authority and commissioned by Christ.

What about people today? There can be no modern day apostle even if a person claims he has seen the resurrected Christ, has been commissioned by Christ, has been taught by Christ, and has the ability to perform miracles in the name of Christ, for he would lack recognition or validation by the other apostles. The twelve chosen by Christ would have to be resurrected from the dead to validate the credentials of a modern day apostle. This is an impossibility, for even if they were raised from the dead, their testimony would contradict Scripture. Scripture testifies to Christ and Christ to the apostles whom He has chosen. Further testimony would reopen Scripture and violate the dictates of God's Word.

God Has Blessed Our Socks Off (1:3-4)

In the original Greek, 1:3-14 constitutes one sentence. Paul was awed and utterly amazed at the blessings of God who blessed us with every spiritual blessing in the heavenly places in Christ (1:3). Paul in his doxology reminds his readers that they share in the new society that is built upon the resurrected Christ. Since Christ is exalted in the heavenly realm, those who are "in Him" also belong to the heavenly realm. Although Christians must live temporarily on earth, their real home is in heaven where spiritual blessings abound. The tension exists between worldly living and heavenly heirship. Paul was amazed that God chose people before the foundation of the earth to be holy and blameless (1:4). But God's election provided the security and the assurance to boldly proclaim the gospel and live only for Christ (Phil. 1:21).

God Is a Choosing God (1:4)

From the beginning of time, God has been a choosing God. Not only did God create Adam as the first man; he chose Adam to be the first, to be humankind's representative. There could not have been a better choice, for God does not make a mistake. No one could have been a better representative. Because Adam was the best choice, all of us suffer death and spiritual separation from God. Our natures became corrupted and depraved as a result of the failure of our representative.

God chose Noah to build an ark to house animals and Noah's family. The ark provided security and protection from the ensuing flood. Only eight people out of all humankind were preserved through the torrential rains and rushing floods. And through Noah and his descendants came further selections of men.

Abraham was chosen from among all the men in the world to be the father of many families who would be blessed. God chose him to receive promises of land and greatness. Abraham did nothing to merit God's favor. Yet, through him God has blessed many nations because the redemption of mankind arose through his seed.

The seed came through the generations of Isaac, whom God chose over Ishmael. From the sons of Isaac, God chose Jacob over Esau. Jacob's son Judah was chosen among the twelve to produce the line of David, from which eventually came the Messiah. David was chosen from among the sons of Jesse to be king. God has always been a choosing God. Why He chooses whom He does, no one knows, but He is sovereign, and He can choose whom He wishes.

Paul saw that, before time as we know it began, God purposed to do something. That purpose concerned Christ, His only begotten Son, and certain created human beings whom He gave to Christ (John 17:9). As God chose Israel out of all the nations of the world,

He also chose a special people to be united with Christ according to the kind intention of His will (1-4), which He exercised in precreation eternity. The doctrine of election is a divine revelation substantiated in the Bible. No biblical Christian can ignore it, although he may profess ignorance in understanding it. Believers cannot reject it, for it is a biblical truth.

God is choosing a community of believers to be separated unto Himself. Left to ourselves, this would never happen, for none of us is good, not even one (Rom. 3:12). None of us is righteous and, therefore, none of us would seek after God (Rom. 3:10-11). If we have all sinned and fallen short of the glory of God (Rom. 3:23), how then could we exercise our minds to select God? We couldn't! Because of our corrupted nature, we would always choose anything but the good, that is, the Ultimate Good. When Adam fell, we all fell with him. Just as Adam lost the ability to choose the proper good, we also lost this ability. We would, therefore, exercise our wills to choose the greatest desire we had at the time, but our desire would never be for God, for we were dead in our transgressions (Eph. 2:1; Col. 2:13). God must have chosen for us; he created some vessels for wrath and some for mercy (Rom. 9:22-23). Since all of us deserve damnation because of our sinfulness, God in His mercy chose to pluck some out of the pit of hell. Others experience His justice and feel the fires of eternal wrath.

What About Free Will?

Does God's choosing us mean that we have no choice in the matter of rejecting or accepting Him? God's grace is irresistible. If He breathes His Spirit into us, we will exercise our wills to choose Him, for we have been created to glorify Him and enjoy Him forever. Once the Spirit comes into us, we will recognize the purpose of our creation, and seeing the ugliness of our sin, we will repent and follow Christ. But the urge to accept Christ comes from God who in love predestined us to adoption as sons and daughters (1:5). God freely bestowed His grace upon us (1:6), which means that we had nothing to do with it. It was not because He foresaw us choosing Him, for we did not have that ability. Nor did He see something acceptable in us, for we are all unrighteous creatures.

Through the shed blood of Christ we have redemption and the forgiveness of our sins (1:7). This does not mean that we never had free will, for we were and still are allowed to choose freely and make decisions. The problem is that we always make decisions that seem to benefit ourselves, often out of self-gratification or self-interest. We exercise our wills to obtain the greatest good or desire we feel at the time. Election doesn't hamper or abrogate free will. On the contrary, it is the culmination and fulfillment of free will. At our rebirth we exercise, through the grace of God, the greatest desire with which we have been created (glorifying and enjoying God).

The doctrine of election gives us an incentive to freely choose holiness, which includes witnessing for Christ. The doctrine gives us strong assurance of eternal salvation, since He who chose us will preserve us until the culmination of history (Phil. 1:6). This is the reason for election: that we be holy and blameless. We become holy as we continually exercise our wills to be as God chose us to be, that is, Christ-like. The lives of those who seek to emulate the Christ who has indwelt them verify God's predestinating love. Therefore, anyone who claims to be one of God's elect and says in his heart, "I'm saved and do not need to bother about seeking holiness," is gravely mistaken and in rebellion to God's call for holiness.

Adoption (1:5-8)

God predestined us to adoption as sons through Jesus Christ (1:5). Why? To show His grace which He freely bestowed upon us (1:6). We certainly did not deserve His grace, but because God is merciful, He provided a way for our sins to be forgiven—through the suffering of Christ (1:7), who became sin itself (II Cor. 5:21) and took upon Himself the wrath we all deserved. In this way God showed us His grace, which would never have been known or experienced if Adam had not fallen. Why then can't all be saved? Because we would never understand God's holiness or His justice.

Who are the children of God? Many people have the mistaken belief that everybody is a child of God. Yet, Scripture tells us that God had only one begotten Son (John 3:16). If a person is not born again, he has no right to be called a child of God. Even if God elected him unto salvation, he does not become a natural son, but rather an adopted child (1:5). To become an adopted child, one must be led by the Spirit of God (Rom. 8:14). If we do become children by adoption, then we also become heirs of God and fellowheirs with Christ (Rom. 8:17), which entitles us to an inheritance foreordained by God (1:11). Yet, to partake of this glorious inheritance, we must suffer with Christ (Rom. 8:17).

If a person is not born of God, whose child is he? Jesus said to the Pharisees that they were doing the work of their father, the devil (John 8:44). This indicates that a person is a child of whom he or she obeys. If a person walks according to the ways of the world, he is a son of the evil one (Eph. 2:2). "Anyone who does not practice righteousness is not of God" (I John 3:10).

But wait a minute! Did not Jesus Himself say that we are all gods according to Scripture (John 10:34)? Jesus was defending His claim that He was the Son of God (John 10:36). The Jews had sought to stone Him for this affirmation. Jesus, therefore, referred to Psalm 82:6, in which Asaph says, "You are gods, and all of you are sons of the Most High." Jesus quoted this to show the Jews the inconsistency of their thinking. How could they stone Him for claiming sonship when Scripture says they are all gods or sons of the Most High?

Some people use this Scripture to claim all human beings are gods or can seek to become gods. Yet, Asaph in Psalm 82 does not mean that we are all literally gods. He wrote the psalm to rebuke unjust judgments and condemn the Israelites who presumptuously thought that their "chosenness" entitled them to do what they pleased to the detriment of the weak and needy. "You're so secure," implied Asaph, "that you think you are gods. Yet, you will die like men." The psalm has a tone of mockery and contempt of those who falsely presume they are secure in the protection of God. Asaph does not mean that the "high and mighty" Israelites are gods. They think they are gods because their inconsiderate behavior and unjust treatment of others have been left unchallenged. Judgment, however, is befalling them, and they will die like ordinary men, for their action has not been missed by God.

The Mystery Unveiled (1:9-12)

The term "mystery" (1:9) recurs in 3:3, 4, 9; 5:32; and 6:19. Here as in other places in the New Testament it means the revelation of a truth that was once unknown. God has chosen to make known to us according to His kind intention (1:9) His plan of salvation, which was conceived in Christ and fulfilled by Him in His ministry on earth. This plan of redemption will culminate at the fulness of time when all things will be summed up under the headship of Christ (1:10). The universe will be in complete harmony and no longer will there be discordant elements. Spiritual warfare will cease, and all those in Christ will possess their inheritance.

This inheritance will include both Jew and Gentile. Verse 11 speaks to the Gentiles who were also predestined according to God's purpose to partake of God's inheritance. They were given a heritage as were the Jews, who first hoped in Christ (1:12). To have both Jew and Gentile equally partaking in the blessing of God which is Christ Jesus is a major reconciliation.

The Seal (1:13-14)

Having believed in Christ, the Jew or the Gentile becomes sealed by the Holy Spirit (1:13), who is given as a pledge of the inheritance promised by God (1:14). What does it mean to be sealed? The word "seal" in Greek is *sphragis*, which has three meanings: one, a signet affixed to a document guaranteeing its authenticity or genuineness; two, a stamp attached to shipped goods proving ownership; three, a sign representing a certain office held in the service of the government. Sealing by the Spirit indicates that a believer belongs to God. It is "proof positive" that he is one of God's elect. However, as one who is sealed, the believer has a responsibility to fulfill the office to which he has been called—that of adopted son (1:5). Those sealed must now serve their Father by obeying Him and witnessing to others of the glory and blessings that have been bestowed upon them. Proof of being sealed, therefore, becomes evident by the fruits of one's life. A person who is a possession of God will depend upon God's will and live for His glory.

Application of Ephesians 1:1-14

1. Although we are not apostles, God does have a purpose for all of us. Where do you believe God is sending you forth this week as a minister in His name? _____

   As one called forth in the authority of Christ, I will not fear, but will serve (name) _____ by (doing) _____.

   Applied: Yes _____ No _____

2. As an adopted child of God, I will experience heavenly glory. Yet, I am thankful for His grace each day. I can show my thankfulness by forgiving others. I know I have a problem with _____ _____ (person). I will therefore seek to rectify the situation by (doing) _____ _____.

   Applied: Yes _____ No _____

Questions for Ephesians 1:15-23

1. In 1:1-14, Paul gives thanks and glory to the Lord for the abundant blessings He bestowed upon the believers. In 1:15, Paul begins his prayer for wisdom and revelation for his readers in the knowledge of God. What is the difference between wisdom and knowledge?

2. What knowledge is Paul speaking about in 1:17? Why then does Paul pray for revelation as well as wisdom?

   a.

b.

3. Paul proposes three things that spiritual people learn. What are
   they? See 1:18-19.

   a.

   b.

   c.

4. What is the chief demonstration of God's love and God's power?

   a. Romans 5:8

   b. Ephesians 1:19-20

3

The Prayer for Knowledge
1:15-23

The Intercession (1:15-17)

After Paul blesses God for choosing us in Christ, he prays that his readers may grasp the fulness of God's riches through Christ Jesus. Having heard of the faith of the Asian Christians (1:15), Paul gives thanks for them (1:16) and prays that God may give them a spirit of wisdom and of revelation in the knowledge of Christ (1:17). Wisdom and revelation cannot be received apart from Christ, who is wisdom (Isa. 11:2) and truth (John 8:44). We cannot possess knowledge of Christ unless the Lord chooses to make Himself known. Hence, Paul prays for revelation in order that his readers may personally know Him who is the spirit of wisdom and understanding, the spirit of counsel and strength, and the spirit of knowledge (Isa. 11:2).

Wisdom and Knowledge (1:17-18)

Paul's prayer for wisdom and revelation is similar to his other recorded prayers. In Colossians 1:9 he prays for his readers to have spiritual wisdom and understanding. In Philippians 1:9 he prays for real knowledge and discernment. Paul is always concerned that the saints grow in the knowledge of Christ, which produces growth in holiness. The highest knowledge one can obtain is to know God personally. This knowledge, however, is impossible unless God Himself chooses to reveal it.

What, then, is the difference between wisdom (*sophia*) and knowledge (*epignōsis*)? When we think of wisdom in the modern sense, we think of "having understanding, common sense, or advanced learning." Although Paul wrote in Greek, his concept of wisdom comes from a Hebrew perspective. The Septuagint, a Greek translation of the Old Testament, uses *sophia* for the Hebrew word *chakas*, which more appropriately means "clever, prudent, and competent for the purpose of functional conduct." Wisdom is insight or perception into the nature of things that leads one to action or use of knowledge gained. Knowledge, on the other hand, is the absorption of things perceived or learned. *Epignōsis* refers to the detection, noting, or recognition of facts or truths. A person may know many things and claim to be an authority in many areas. Yet, without wisdom, knowledge makes one arrogant (I Cor. 8:1) and can even become dangerous.

Wisdom gives knowledge its proper perspective and is the catalyst for putting one's knowledge to meaningful action. Wisdom is the ability to activate knowledge in a sensible and competent manner. The Hebrew concept emphasizes experience more than understanding. The Greek has in mind absorbing facts and cataloging information rather than using the information. Paul prays that his readers would not just retain facts about God, but rather that their hearts (1:18) would experience God personally. Paul speaks about the highest knowledge obtainable—the knowledge of God Himself.

The Eyes of the Heart (1:18-19)

Scripture normally refers to the heart not only as the base for emotion, but also as the seat of intelligence, of moral thought, and of will. In order for a person to activate his knowledge about God, he needs a vision (or eyes to see) to understand God's reality and transcendence. The Holy Spirit must illuminate (enlighten) this vision (1:18) for a person to possess wisdom in knowing God, in grasping His revealed truth, and in realizing God's eternal purpose and plan for His chosen ones.

Those whom He enlightens, the Holy Spirit also instructs in three things from God's revelation. First, they learn what the hope of their calling is. The call of God is grounded in His choice from the foundation of the earth (1:4). Those "whom He predestined, these

He also called; and whom He called, these He also justified" (Rom. 8:30). Yes, we do call upon Him to save us (Rom. 10:12-13), but our coming to Him is merely an irresistible response to His urgings.

What in the world would God call us for? Contrary to what we might believe, God has a great purpose for us. He does not issue calls arbitrarily. That is why Paul prays that we might know the "hope of our calling." We need the Spirit, however, to grant us discernment in order to understand and seek God's plan for our lives. Once we do personally know the Lord, we must submit and commit our works to Him. If we do this, our plans will be established (Prov. 16:3). Our plans, however, must be grounded in His call, which is holy (II Tim. 1:9). Since we were called to belong to Jesus Christ and to partake of His fellowship (I Cor. 1:9), we must separate ourselves as a holy people, for God is holy (I Pet. 1:15; Lev. 11:44).

Second, believers learn of the riches of the glory of God's inheritance (1:18). Whose inheritance is Paul talking about? Is it God's inheritance, that is, the inheritance He receives, or is it our inheritance, that is, the inheritance God bestows? The Greek reading of this passage could mean either one. Some commentators believe the first rendering is correct, for God's people constitute His inheritance or possession. Certainly the Old Testament teaches this concept, and it is consistent with 1:14. Others believe the second view is correct, for it parallels Colossians 1:12, which suggests that the saints are qualified to share in the inheritance that God graciously bestows upon those who belong to Christ. In either case, as God's possession or Christ's co-heirs, we will still experience the blessings of eternal reward.

Third, Paul wants us to learn the surpassing greatness of God's power (1:19). In order to understand God's call, the saint must look backward toward election, which is from the foundation of the earth. To understand God's inheritance, the believer must focus on the culmination of history and heavenly rewards. In other words, a believer has been taught to look at the beginning and at the end, but what happens in between? What does a Christian focus upon in the interim? Paul answers this by praying for the saints to be enlightened in the knowledge of God's power, for it is His surpassing power that spans the period from election to inheritance. Only God's power can maintain the believer from the call to repent (becoming born again) to the call to glory where the riches of his inheritance await.

Paul is utterly convinced of the sufficiency of God's power. In order to convince his readers, he draws upon all the synonyms he can accumulate to describe the exceeding greatness of God's power. He speaks of the immeasurable energy (working) of God's great strength and might (1:19). A believer who concentrates on God's might should have no fear in performing the acts of sanctification that proceed from God's saving act.

The Demonstration of God's Power (1:20-23)

God has given a public demonstration of His power by raising Jesus Christ from the dead and exalting Him in the heavenly places (1:20). Because He is seated at the Father's right hand, Christ is far above all rule and authority (1:21). No one on earth from any age can compare or compete with Him.

The power of Christ's resurrection also demonstrates God's love, because in order for the resurrection to have occurred, Christ had to experience death for all of us. God shows His "love toward us, in that while we were yet sinners, Christ died for us" (Rom. 5:8). Christ was not only raised from the dead, He was made head over all things for the church (1:22). The church (community of believers) is the new society that God has called into being. God appointed Christ as supreme head and ruler of this new society, the individual members of which constitute His body (1:23). The conception of the church as Christ's body is a Pauline illustration. In some of Paul's earlier letters (Romans and Corinthians), he develops the idea of believers' functioning separately with their God-given gifts, yet harmoniously and in unison as one body, the body of Christ (Rom. 12:4-5; I Cor. 12:12).

The church is not an institution but a vital organism that exists and functions by reason of the resurrected Christ. The church as a body derives its lifeblood from its head, Christ Jesus. The church is a sorry sight today, for the body of believers is more a picture of a quadriplegic. The head sends signals to move and to perform, but the body lies paralyzed and immovable.* The church, however, has been called to experience the fulness of Christ (1:23), who is the fulness of Deity dwelling in bodily form (Col. 2:9). This is exciting, for the church as a body is the fulness or complement to its head. Since the church is the complement of Christ, it must actively perform the dictates of the head. Hence, it is important to understand the power of God, because the power that raised Christ from the dead is the same power that works within believers (3:20). It is the power to turn from sin, to walk with Christ, and to build up other parts of the body in preparing them as effective witnesses and warriors for Christ.

Application of Ephesians 1:15-23

1. I will obtain the highest knowledge possible, which is to know God personally. I will set apart _____ minutes per day to have a quiet time to read and meditate upon God's Word.

Applied: Yes _____ No _____

2. I am convinced of my inheritance with God and am assured of my salvation. Because I am convicted and assured of the sufficiency of God's grace and power, I will share my faith this week with _____.

Applied: Yes _____ No _____

If I am not convinced, I will seek counsel with _____ _____ to discuss my insecurities.

Applied: Yes _____ No _____

---

* This illustration is not meant to be offensive. The author's cousin is a born again Christian who as a result of a diving accident has been paralyzed for the past fifteen years. He is a beautiful Christian who has helped the author see the church in a paralyzed state.

Questions for Ephesians 2:1-10

1. What does it mean to be dead in our trespasses and sins (2:1)? How were we made alive (2:5)?

    a.

    b.

2. If we are saved by grace as a gift of God (2:8), how do we answer the critics who say that Jesus commended people for their faith? Doesn't this show that faith is an individual choice and not a gift?

3. What does it mean to be God's workmanship (2:10)? What, then, is the evidence of the power of a new life?

    a.

    b.

4

The Resurrection Power

———————— *2:1-10* ————————

Dead in Trespasses (2:1-5)

In 1:20, Paul explained God's power by reminding us that He raised Christ from the dead. Not only was raising Christ a display of God's mighty power, but so also is the raising of Christ's people (2:5-6), who were dead in their trespasses and sins (2:1). This deadness is a universal human condition. Of course, Paul is speaking about spiritual death, for outside of Christ there is no life. Death has occurred because of our ungodliness and inability to do good (Rom. 3:12). We have trespassed (*paraptōma*), or deviated from the proper path, and sinned (*hamartia*), or missed the mark. In other words, we have fallen short of the glory of God (Rom. 3:23) by commission (transgressing) and by omission (falling short of God's standard). The result is alienation, or spiritual separation from God, for the wages of sin are death (Rom. 6:23).

When we walked in accordance with worldly principles, we followed the dictates of Satan (2:2). We had no desire or inclination to give our lives to Christ. In fact, because we were dead, we had no ability to make a decision for Christ. What, then, is wrong with this common illustration used by many evangelists?

> We are all drowning in the sea of disobedience and worldly pleasures. The evangelist approaches in a boat preaching about Christ the Savior. He throws us a life preserver, Jesus. All we have to do to be saved is grab the life preserver, that is, latch on to Jesus Christ.

The problem with this illustration is that the nonbeliever is not drowning. He has already drowned (spiritually), for he is dead in trespasses and sins (2:1). How can someone who is dead reach up and grab a life preserver? He cannot. He first needs God to breathe His Spirit into him, to make him alive with Christ (2:5). God's breath is given graciously and mercifully to those He has chosen from the beginning (1:1). Why? Because of His great love for us (2:4). Why He chose us to believe is an unanswerable question, for we surely did not deserve His favor. However, by God's grace (2:5) we are able to grab the life preserver and, thereby, exercise faith in Christ. We may think we are choosing Christ by our own volition, but our volition is the result of an irresistible urge to do so (Rom. 1:6-7; I Cor. 1:2, 18). God called us a chosen race, a holy people (I Pet. 2:9). And those He calls, He also justifies, and those He justifies, He also glorifies (Rom. 8:30). The gospel invitation is truly extended to all who hear the message. Yet, this outward and general call will not bring everyone to Christ, for the unregenerate are dead in their sins and unable and unwilling to forsake their evil and worldly ways. The elect, because God so desired, will have the scales lifted from their eyes and plugs removed from their ears in order to respond to God's call. This is what Christ meant when He said many are called, but few are chosen (Matt. 22:14). The general invitation goes to all who hear the gospel, but only the elect respond to the call.

The Supreme Demonstration of Grace (2:6-7)

In 1:19 Paul comments on the surpassing greatness of God's power evidenced in His raising Christ from the dead (1:20). In a similar fashion, the raising of the people of Christ to be seated with Him in the heavenly places (2:6) is the supreme demonstration of God's grace (2:7). As children of wrath (3:1), we (Gentiles and Jews alike) surely did not merit God's favor. To be a child of wrath, one is necessarily an enemy of God. God's wrath is never arbitrary but rather is His personal hostility toward evil. God does not compromise with evil, nor with our lustful indulgences (2:3), but instead condemns them. In order to demonstrate the riches of His mercy (2:7), God sent Christ to die for us (John 3:16). Christ's sacrifice, His propitiation for our sins (I John 4:10), was the ultimate demonstration of God's grace toward us.

The Gift of Salvation (2:8-9)

"But God" (2:4) are two words that carry the entire meaning of grace, for these two monosyllables indicate God's initiative and action on behalf of fallen mankind. Left to our own sinful selves, we would remain captive to the desires of the flesh and the mind (2:3). We were dead (2:1,5), "but God" made us alive (2:5). We were slaves to our passions (2:3) and to the evil one (2:2), "but God" seated us with Christ as a heavenly inheritance (2:6).

What, then, is God's grace? In one word, it is "salvation." For it is by grace that we have been saved through faith (2:8). The Greek word for "saved" is *sesōsmenoi*, a participle in the perfect tense. The perfect tense in Greek indicates an action completed in the past that has continuing effect in the present and the future. *Sesōsmenoi* emphasizes a completed saving act, the effect of which has abiding consequences. In other words, Paul gives assurance of salvation by saying in effect, "You people have been saved by God's grace and, therefore, remain forever saved."

But if we are saved through faith, doesn't this mean that we exercise faith? And if so, doesn't it mean that we have a part in our own salvation? Many people mistakenly believe they have a part to play in their own salvation. True, once saved, they exercise their faith in serving the Lord, for without works their faith is dead and useless (James 2:17,20). Faith is the assurance of things hoped for, the conviction of things not seen (Heb. 11:1). One could never gain assurance by his own works (Rom. 10:3). Assurance is obtained only through the work of righteousness (Isa. 32:17), which is Christ Himself. Since all our righteousness is as filthy rags (Isa. 64:6), we could never do anything pleasing to God prior to His breathing His Spirit into us. That is why God imputes Christ's righteousness to us. In order for a holy God to look upon us sinful creatures, He must first clothe us in the righteousness of His Son. And this is God's gift to us (2:8).

Once allowed by God, we can then appropriate His gift of salvation unto ourselves. Appropriation is by the exercise of our faith, but faith does not precede the gift. Otherwise, choosing God by grasping the gift would be an example of our own works. Paul tells us that salvation, which is deliverance from death, slavery, and wrath (2:1-3), is not a result of our works, which would give us the right to boast (2:9). There are no prideful people in heaven, only those who are thankful for God's grace. Grace is the antithesis of works, for if salvation "is by grace, it is no longer on the basis of works, otherwise grace is no longer grace" (Rom. 11:6).

God's Workmanship (2:10)

Although we are not saved *by* our own religious deeds or philanthropic works, we are saved *for* good works (2:10). God fashioned us into a new creation "in Christ Jesus." We become God's work of art and are displayed by the works we perform. Our salvation becomes evident by the way we walk in the works that God has preordained for us (2:10). As a new creation (I Cor. 5:17), we are not passive or inert. God's election and grace do not encourage passivity or sinfulness. On the contrary, we must actively demonstrate God's gift of salvation by performing good works and continuously walking in them (James 2:18).

Application of Ephesians 2:1-10

1. Because God was gracious to me, I too will be gracious to _____
   _____, a nonbeliever, and take him/her out to lunch this week.

   Applied: Yes _____ No _____

2. I understand that God saved me in order that I may perform good works. I will, therefore, (do) _____
   _____this week and give God the glory.

   Applied: Yes _____ No _____

Questions for Ephesians 2:11-22

1. Why does God constantly ask us to remember our alienation (2:11-12)?

2. What union is Paul talking about in 2:14? Verse 15 says the union came about by Christ's abolishing the enmity, which is the law. How can this be when Christ Himself said that He did not come to abolish the law, but to fulfill it?

   a.

   b.

3. When you think of peace (2:17), what do you mean? Compare your definition with the Aaronic benediction in Numbers 6:24-26. How did the Hebrews view peace?

   a.

   b.

4. In 2:20, does "foundation" mean that laid by the prophets and apostles or does it mean the prophets and apostles themselves? (See I Cor. 3:11 and Eph. 3:5.)

5

The New Society

Remember (2:11-12)

In 2:1-10 Paul dealt with the moral condition of the Gentiles prior to God's breathing His Spirit into them. Because God was rich in mercy (2:4), He made alive (2:5) and saved those whom He had chosen from the foundation of the world (1:4) by grace (2:8), so that none could boast (2:9). The Gentiles were not only dead in their trespasses and sins, but also disadvantaged by being outside the "circumcision" (2:11), that is, the commonwealth of Israel. They should remember their former state (2:11), which did not contain the covenants of promise or the hope of God's eternal presence (2:12).

Paul emphasizes the alienation of man from God. "Remember that you were at that time separate from Christ" (2:12). Not only is man disaffected from God, he is also estranged from other human beings. The second part of chapter 2 depicts the breakdown of fundamental human relationships.

But why does Paul want his readers to remember their alienation? Most people would consider this type of remembrance distasteful and would want to hide it in the recesses of their minds, never to bring it up. Yet, a constant reminder of where we were apart from God's grace is necessary if we are to appreciate what He has done for us and to keep us from pridefully thinking we are something special. Remembering our past outside of Christ means remembering how wretched and ungodly we were. If it were not for the loving intervention of God through the blood of Christ, we would still be delightfully walking in the deeds of the flesh: immorality, impurity, sensuality, idolatry, sorcery, enmities, strife, jealousy, outbursts of anger, disputes, dissensions, factions, envyings, drunkenness, carousings, and other like things (Gal. 5:19-21). God knows we need to look back and see the ugliness of our former ways, for without retrospection we tend to forget how and what we were to our own prideful detriment. Moses and the prophets constantly had to remind the Israelites of their deliverance by God from the hands of the Egyptians. Without the reminder, the Israelites soon fell into apathy and became content in their own ways. At the Last Supper, Jesus broke bread and took wine and told the apostles to do likewise in memory of Him (Luke 22:19). Partaking of the Lord's Supper demonstrates God's grace toward us in that it proclaims the Lord's death until He comes (I Cor. 11:26), during which time we are strengthened against sin, supported in tribulation, encouraged to serve, and inspired to love. Without this constant reminder of the Lord's death, we would be quick to deny His existence, His atonement, and His lordship.

The New Humanity (2:12-15)

Paul also reminds his Gentile readers that they were excluded from the earlier community of God's people (Israel). If you were not an Israelite, you were a stranger to God's covenantal promises (2:12). The sign of entrance into the covenantal community was circumcision (Gen. 17:10-14). The Jews boasted that they were the circumcised of God and, therefore, inheritors of the Abrahamic blessings. They even went to the extreme of contemptuously nicknaming the Gentiles (the religiously underprivileged) "the Uncircumcision" (2:11). Paul, however, does not use the term in a derogatory fashion. In fact, he calls the Jews the "so-called Circumcision." As a Jew, Paul attacks those who claim to be spiritually important because of some outward act. Circumcision is a manmade mark that holds no spiritual significance, for the real circumcision is of the heart (Ezek. 36:26). "Be sure," says Paul, "that it is those who are of faith that are sons of Abraham" (Gal. 3:7), not those who are ritually circumcised.

Although Paul outlines the former state of the Gentiles, he is eager to establish their ingrafting into the community of faith. "But now in Christ Jesus you who formerly were far off have been brought near by the blood of Christ" (2:13). Paul turns their attention from desolation without Christ to joy with Christ. Use of the historical name "Jesus" emphasizes that the anticipated Jewish Messiah and Savior of all is fulfilled in the person and work of a man called Jesus. The work of Christ Jesus was His death and resurrection and was performed for the elect of God, whether Jew or Gentile.

The Jew during this period had immense contempt for Gentiles. He would call them not only the "uncircumcised," but also dogs. He considered the Gentiles objects of God's wrath. A Jew was not allowed to help any of them, even in time of dire need. If a Jew had the audacity to marry from among the *goyyim*, the community ostracized him or her and even held a funeral. Paul grew up with this hatred and contempt. But now he says that God's grace through Christ touches even the Gentiles, for in Christ there is no Jew or Gentile (Gal. 3:28). Whether a person is circumcised or not means absolutely nothing (Gal. 5:6).

God is building a new humanity that includes reconciliation between the Jew and the Gentile. Through Christ He makes both groups into one, having broken down the dividing wall (2:14). If we are to be at peace with God, we must be at peace with one another. Nothing short of the gospel can break down barriers that polarize mankind into hostile factions. Some commentators believe that Paul had a literal wall in mind when he wrote verse 14, the wall of the temple in Jerusalem separating the court of the Gentiles from the courts of the priests and Israelites. The court was spacious and ran completely around the three inner courts. From anywhere within the court, a Gentile could look up and see the temple, but he was not allowed to enter it or the other courts upon fear of death.

The wall representing the enmity between Jew and Gentile was abolished by Christ's sacrificing His body on the cross (2:15). The hatred and separation between the two antagonists was also represented by the "law of commandments contained in ordinances" (2:15). This Christ also abrogated by His atoning act. But how can Paul say that Christ abolished the law when Christ Himself specifically said He did not come to abolish the law but to fulfill it (Matt.

5:17)? The discrepancy or inconsistency is only verbal, for a deeper look at the context of each statement clearly shows there is no contradiction. In the Sermon on the Mount, Jesus taught the difference between righteousness as viewed by the Pharisees and righteousness as meant by God. He referred to the moral law, which governs one's attitude and obedience to the dictates of God. Christ fulfilled the moral law by perfectly obeying and following it. This law has not been abolished as a standard of behavior; it is still valid and binding on the followers of Christ. As we seek to love and emulate Christ, we submit ourselves to the moral law. Yet, if this law were the way to salvation or to the attainment of God, then in reality it would become a barrier between us and God. Christ abolished this barrier or view of the law, for He is the only way to God. He is salvation itself. Nothing we can do will merit us eternal life. No one but the God-man Christ can grant us the free gift of life with God.

In 2:15, Paul is not talking specifically about the moral law. He refers to the ceremonial laws ("the law of commandments contained in ordinances"). These laws were the great dividing factor between Jew and Gentile. Circumcision was the main physical difference between the two groups. Other rules and regulations separating them concerned sacrifices, ritual cleanness, dietary regulations, and celebrations of Sabbath and festivals. Paul in his companion letter to the Colossians also alludes to the same rules and regulations (Col. 2:11, 16-21). These ceremonial commandments and ordinances became the divisive wall between the Jew and Gentile. It was this barrier that Christ tore down. His sacrifice on the cross fulfilled all the types and shadows in the Old Testament that were represented by the ceremonial law. This law Christ did abolish in His flesh in order that the two groups (Jew and Gentile) might be made into one new humanity, thus establishing peace (2:15).

Shalom *(2:16-18)*

Christ's sacrificial death provided the way to reconciliation between Jew and Gentile (2:16), for His atoning death culminated His ministry on earth, when He preached peace (2:17) to those who were far away (Gentiles) and to those who were near (Jews). By proclaiming peace, Christ fulfilled Isaiah 52:6: "Therefore, My people shall know My name; therefore in that day I am the one who is speaking, 'Here I am.'" And how did He present Himself? By proclaiming good news and announcing peace (Isa. 52:7).

When he wrote the word "peace," Paul, a Hebrew, would have been thinking *shalom*, the Hebrew word for peace and a derivative of *shalam*, which means to be safe in mind, body, and estate. In other words, *shalom* means to be whole or complete and includes health, prosperity, peacefulness, and rightness with God. Even to this day, when an Israelite says, *"Ma shalomha,"* ("How are you?"), he is asking, "How is the peace within you?" He is asking if you are whole or complete today, or if some facet of your life is hurting. The Aaronic benediction in Numbers 6:24-26 speaks to this wholeness. May "the Lord bless you [grant you prosperity], and keep you [protect you]; the Lord make His face shine on you [make you right with Him], and be gracious to you [grant you favor]; the Lord lift up His countenance on you [keep you in health] and give you peace [keep you from conflict within the family, community, and nation]."

Christ is our peace offering (Lev. 3:1-2), our *shalom* (John 16:33), and our wholeness. Without Christ, there is no peace and, therefore, no access in one Spirit to the Father (2:18), for He is the way, the truth, and the life, and no one can come to the Father except through Him (John 14:8). So then, Gentiles and Jews alike who are believers in Christ are at peace with each other and are members of the same household of faith. No longer are Gentiles "strangers and aliens," but they are now "fellow-citizens with the saints" (2:19), "having been built upon the foundation of the apostles and prophets, Christ Jesus Himself being the corner stone" (2:20).

The Foundation (2:19-22)

In 2:19, Paul uses images of citizenship and family. His Gentile readers are "fellow citizens" and are "of God's household." Paul adds a third image, that of a building (2:20) and, more particularly, a temple (2:21). To be a citizen in God's kingdom and a member of His household, one had to receive a faith "built upon the foundation of the apostles and prophets" (2:20). Is the foundation that which was laid by the apostles and prophets or the apostles and prophets themselves? In I Corinthians 3:11, Paul says, "No man can lay a foundation other than the one which is laid, which is Jesus Christ." Is Paul now contradicting himself by saying the foundation is that of the apostles and prophets? No! The foundation Paul speaks about in verse 20 is not the apostles or prophets themselves. It is not the office of apostle or prophet that constitutes the basis of our faith. Rather, the basis of faith is Christ Jesus. The apostles and prophets were to teach that faith and to propagate the gospel. Since both groups had a teaching function, we accept them as God's inspired professors and vessels of divine revelation (3:5). It seems clear, therefore, that their instruction, not their personages, constitutes the foundation of the church.

The church is built upon the Scriptures, which were written by men who were moved by the Holy Spirit (II Pet. 1:21), and Jesus Christ holds the Scriptures together, for the Old Testament points to Him and the New Testament testifies of Him. Christ is the corner-stone (2:20) in whom the whole building (our faith) fits together as a holy temple in the Lord (2:22). Paul uses the metaphor of the temple for a number of reasons. First, he illustrates the new home of God. No longer does God dwell in a building, nor is He to be represented by a superstructure. Rather, He dwells with His people who become the temple of His Holy Spirit (I Cor. 3:16). This breaks down the final barrier between Jew and Gentile. The Gentile who had no access to the Jewish temple now becomes a temple himself through belief in Jesus Christ.

Second, Paul shows the importance of a cornerstone. It is part of and essential to the entire foundation. It holds the building together. It supports the weight of the structure and serves as the measure for architectural exactness. Christ, who holds all things together (Col. 1:17), is the cornerstone of our faith (I Pet. 2:6). If we add to or take away from the cornerstone (Christ), we weaken the building and erect a new measuring standard that violates the architect's original design and purpose. The building (church) as a living organism continuing to grow (2:21) will cave in if it does not loyally stand on the foundational truths revealed through the apostles and prophets. That happened to Judaism and its temple worship. The Jews rejected the cornerstone (Ps. 118:22) and stumbled over it (Isa. 8:14), and consequently experienced dispersion.

Third, Paul shows the fulfillment of prophecy in Christ. Christ was the choice stone laid in Zion (Isa. 28:16). Anyone who believes in Him as the precious cornerstone of faith will not be disappointed (I Pet. 2:6). Christ, however, was the stone the builders (Jews) did reject (Ps. 118:22) but that stone became the very cornerstone of the faith. As the stone rejected, Christ became a stumbling block (Isa. 8:14) and a rock of offense for those who are disobedient to the Word (I Pet. 2:8) and to the instructions of the apostles and prophets. Without belief in Christ, one cannot be built into the community of faith and become a vessel for the living Lord (2:22).

Application of Ephesians 2:11-22

1. God teaches us to be unified as a body of believers. To foster this unity, I will get together with the following believers for dinner on _____ (date): _____
_____.

Applied: Yes _____ No _____

2. God has formed a new humanity in Christ Jesus. I realize that I am a new creature in Christ, but I still need to improve many areas of my life to become more Christ-like. I will, therefore, change _____ (something in my life) this week in order to show people around me that I am more Christ-like.

Applied: Yes _____ No _____

Questions for Ephesians 3:1-13

1. Ephesians 3:2 speaks of the administration or stewardship of God's grace. Some translators have called it a dispensation of God's grace. This word choice has led others to believe that God has ordained various dispensations throughout the ages, the present one—from Christ's death to His second coming—being

the period of grace. Why does Paul say that *he* was given the administration or stewardship of God's grace (3:8; Acts 9)? Why is this important (3:5-6)?

a.

b.

2. What is the mystery that was hidden in God (3:9)? See Colossians 1:26-27. Why do you suppose God chose to reveal it through Paul (I Cor. 1:26-31)?

a.

b.

3. Why do you suppose the church is important (3:10)? How does this stand against the view that a personal relationship to Christ is all a person needs?

a.

b.

6

Paul's Stewardship

_____ *3:1-13* _____

The Prisoner (3:1)

Paul in 2:11-22 reminded us that once in Christ Jesus, we become part of the new humanity that God has preordained since the beginning of time. As a new society, there is no delineation between Jew and Gentile. In Christ, both Jew and Gentile become reconciled as one body to God (2:16) and have one access in one Spirit to the Father (2:18). Paul now tells his readers that he has been given stewardship of God's grace for them (3:2). In so doing, he has become a prisoner of Christ Jesus (3:1).

Paul was not only a spiritual prisoner of Christ, in that he was held captive by God's grace; he was also physically restrained by the Romans. He viewed this imprisonment as also in the service of Christ, especially for the sake of the Gentiles (3:1). It was Paul's faithfulness to Christ that caused him to preach to the Gentiles the good news of their ingrafting into God's household (2:19). And ironically, it was this faithfulness that resulted in hostile Jews' seeking his death. The animosity of his opponents led him to appeal to Roman jurisdiction and eventually resulted in house arrest in Rome under Nero's regime.

Although Paul had appealed to the Emperor of Rome and submitted to his jurisdiction, he never thought of himself as Nero's prisoner. Paul believed in the sovereignty of God and knew that all things worked together for good for those who loved God and were called according to His purpose (Rom. 8:28). What the Jews and the Romans meant for evil, God meant for good (Gen. 50:20). Paul understood this and knew that God ruled in the affairs of men. This is why he called himself a "prisoner of Christ" (3:1) or the "prisoner of the Lord" (4:1). He uses the same expression in Philemon verses 1 and 9, and in II Timothy 1:8. Paul understood that the lordship of Christ covered even his imprisonment. If he was in prison, there must be a purpose for it. During his confinement he wrote letters that reproved, encouraged, and instructed other Christians.

Paul's acceptance of his imprisonment and his infirmities should encourage all of us. We should recognize God's sovereignty and Christ's lordship in all our circumstances no matter how desperate they may seem. God is in control even though we may not think so. Our job is to submit to Christ's lordship and exercise our wills to follow the Lord even in the face of pain or death. By remembering that our strength is in the joy of the Lord (Neh. 8:10), we will be encouraged to joyously love the Lord and gird ourselves for the spiritual warfare in which we are embroiled.

Paul's Stewardship (3:2-6)

God appointed Paul to administer His grace (3:2) by proclaiming to the Gentiles the good news of Christ's death and resurrection, which provided the way to eternal life. Why would God choose Paul to receive revelation (3:3) and make known the mystery of Christ (3:4), which had not been revealed in other generations (3:5)? Only God knows why He chooses anyone. Explaining why He chose to number Paul among the apostles and prophets (3:5) would be mere speculation. God has always been a choosing God, but He does choose the foolish things of the world to shame the wise and the weak to confound the strong (I Cor. 1:27). Paul admitted that he was a Pharisee and a persecutor of the church (Phil. 3:5-6). As a Pharisee, he probably disdained the Gentiles as the dregs of society. As a persecutor of Christians, he had taken joy in seeing followers of Christ imprisoned and murdered. Paul was an unlikely candidate for apostleship, at least in the eyes of humanity. God, however, had prepared Paul to become the apostle to the Gentiles through education as a Pharisee and through experience as a persecutor. He used all of Paul's training and ability and rechanneled it as His "chosen instrument . . . to bear His name before the Gentiles and kings and the sons of Israel" (Acts 9:15). In so doing, Paul suffered on account of Christ's name and, therefore, experienced the pain of being a Christ-follower (Acts 9:16).

The mystery that Paul speaks about is that Christ's atoning act on the cross was not only for Jews, but also for Gentiles. This means that all of humanity was issued the call to become fellow heirs, fellow members of the body, and fellow partakers of the promise in Christ (3:6). Although the call to salvation is general, only a few are chosen according to Christ's words in Matthew 22:14 (see the earlier discussion of 2:1-5, under "Dead in Trespasses"). Those few would experience "the riches of the glory of this mystery . . . which is Christ in [them]" (Col. 1:27).

Paul's Administration of Grace (3:7-13)

In order to fulfill his stewardship requirements, Paul "was made a minister, according to the gift of God's grace which was given to [him] according to the working of [God's] power" (3:7). That God would choose him, the very least of the saints, to receive grace to preach the riches of God to the Gentiles (3:8) and to reveal the mystery of Christ, which had been formerly hidden in God (3:9), surprised Paul. God selected Paul "to bring to light" the plan He had purposed from all eternity (3:11) and was now unfolding through the ministry of this "apostle to the Gentiles." God was reuniting humanity (Jew and Gentile) and fulfilling the promise He made to Abraham that "in [him] all the families of the earth shall be blessed" (Gen. 12:3).

God desired that His eternal truth and wisdom, Christ Jesus (Isa. 11:2; John 8:44), "be made known through the church to rulers and the authorities in the heavenly places" (3:10). It appears that God's grace, which reunited mankind, had value and purpose for these inhabitants of the heavenly realm as well. As the grace of God spreads to more and more individuals, the Christian community spreads and the story of the church unfolds. The spectators of this drama of salvation are the cosmic beings, "the rulers and authorities of the heavenly places." Since these cosmic intelligences are not omniscient, but long for the knowledge of the good news of salvation (I Pet. 1:12), they have no way of knowing the master plan of God. God, evidently, did not desire to reveal His plan of grace through Christ directly to these "powers and principalities." Rather, He chose to unfold it "through the church." Although we can't see them, they can see us and watch us grow as the body of Christ "in whom we have boldness and confident access through faith in Him" (3:12).

Because Paul has this confidence in God, he can tell his readers not to worry so much about his tribulations (3:13). Some people think today, as possibly some of Paul's readers did, that if a person is really in God's will, he will not experience many trials and tribulations. Life will be peaceful and without conflict. Paul assured his readers that his difficulties and sufferings were for their benefit and their glory (3:13). His hardship would serve as an encouragement to them to persevere through the "valley of the shadow of death" (Ps. 23:4).

The Importance of the Church (3:10)

The first half of Ephesians 3 teaches the importance of the church. Some people would have us believe that the church is worthless, and that a personal relationship to Jesus Christ is all that matters. True, one must have a personal relationship with Christ to be called a Christian. But, having a right relationship means not forsaking the assembling together (Heb. 10:25) and not avoiding fellowship with one another (I John 1:7). Although there are many "dead" churches, which are not subservient to the Lord, we cannot generally condemn the institution of the church, for God has not abandoned it, but rather has chosen it as central to the working out of His eternal purpose (3:10-11).

The church is important for a number of reasons. First, God has ordained the church as central to human history. Yet, if we look in history books in the public schools, the history of the church is hardly mentioned. Instead, we read about kings and kingdoms, presidents and politicians, and wars and warriors. The Bible, God's history, concentrates on the nobodies, the unimportant in the world's eyes. God has chosen these nobodies, however, to become part of the church, the body of Christ. The church as delineated in the Bible becomes a major emphasis in the salvation history God has preordained through Jesus Christ. History is not a random succession of events. It is the moving plan of God. It is not the reporting of wars and territorial annexation, but the expansion of God's endless growing community of believers known as the church. The church existing within the world continues God's plan and emphasizes redemptive history.

Second, the church proclaims the gospel. "Faith comes from hearing and hearing by the word of Christ" (Rom. 10:17). Those believers whom the church comprises are commissioned to plant and to water the seeds of truth. They are to tell the story of Christ's atonement, for how is anyone to believe if he hasn't heard the gospel (Rom. 10:14)? The good news of salvation comes from the midst of a vibrant, growing, and sharing church.

Third, through the church believers support one another and share burdens. There is no such thing as "solo-Christianity." In fact, the New Testament addresses groups of Christians to encourage them individually and corporately to walk together in Christ and not to walk alone. We are called together as God's elect, not only to share our faith and to worship the Lord, but to share in each other's problems and to rejoice in each other's victories. As a part of the body of Christ (Rom. 12:5), we all have our special function in the body's operation (I Cor. 12:14-27). Any believer who forsakes the fellowship deprives the body of a special and functioning part. He will not become part of a support group or know of needs within the body. He becomes as a paralyzed hand that says to the rest of the human body, "I will not aid you anymore, nor do I wish to partake of your functions." Each believer is important to the whole body of Christ and necessary for the proper functioning and mission of the church (I Cor. 12:22).

Fourth, the church is the army of Christ and must fight spiritual battles (Eph. 6:12). Any soldier who ventures out into the battlefield alone will be annihilated through his own stupidity. A soldier knows his duty and function within his unit. He is not so ignorant as to leave the security of his unit and try to defeat the enemy on his own. In the same regard, a believer should not be so foolish as to

a. 3:14

b. 3:15

c. 3:16

d. 3:17

e. 3:18

f. 3:19

g. 3:20

h. 3:21

7

The Identifying Factors of a Mature Christian

3:14-21

Introduction to Prayer (3:14)

Paul resumes the prayer he began in 3:1, "For this reason . . ." What reason (3:14) was in his mind that he once again brings to prayer? In 1:17 he prayed for the impartation of wisdom so that his readers might know the hope of God's calling and the riches of His inheritance in the saints (1:18). Paul now concludes this prayer by bringing to the attention of his readers the qualities and needs of a mature believer in Christ.

Identifying a Mature Christian (3:14-21)

The basis of Paul's prayer was his unshakable belief in the sovereignty of God. He understood the eternal purpose of God (3:11) and the reconciling work of Christ, which recreated a lost society (2:16). No longer was there to be Jew or Gentile, but rather one humanity in Christ (2:14). He prays for this new humanity and by example and petition gives every believer actions to emulate and criteria with which to be identified. For a believer to be a mature Christian, he needs to show eight different traits or qualities found in 3:14-21.

Humility. First, a Christian is humble. "For this reason I bow my knees" (3:14). A Jew normally prayed standing. Kneeling was an unusual posture. Scripture gives no hard and fast rule about what posture one should adopt while praying. However, kneeling demonstrates contriteness, earnestness, and humility. Peter says that we are all to be "clothed with humility . . . for God is opposed to the proud, but gives grace to the humble" (I Pet. 5:5). In a humble position we approach the Father with our petitions and supplications. By humbling ourselves, we will be more in tune to pray in accordance with God's will and motivation, and not our own. We actually have no authority to pray in accordance with our own desires, but rather we are to pray only for those things revealed as God's will, hence the importance of Scripture reading and Bible study, for Scripture is God's revealed will. Prayer is the key to the operation of God's disclosed will. Therefore, Scripture reading and prayer are indispensable partners.

Identification. Second, a mature Christian identifies with God's household (2:19; 3:15). How does one do this? By bowing before the Father (3:14), totally abandoning the self to Him and His wishes. He wishes us to be clothed with the righteousness of Christ (II Cor. 5:21). We, therefore, must give our lives in complete obedience to the Son, whose death made us fellow citizens with the saints (2:14). Many people profess to be part of God's citizenry by stating that Jesus is their Savior because He died for their sins. That is only part of the gospel. Jesus is not Savior to anyone to whom He is not Lord. Christ's lordship means that we must give all of ourselves and all of our actions to the King. If we hold back any part of ourselves or our lives, we demonstrate that we still sit on the throne of our existence. Christ as Savior and Christ as Lord are flip sides of the same coin. You can't have one without the other, for Christ is either Lord of all, or not Lord at all.

Invigoration. Third, a mature Christian demonstrates the power of invigoration. Paul prays that God will strengthen the believer "with power through His Spirit in the inner man" (3:16). A Christian needs to be fortified with the assurance of God's power, not his own. When a believer attempts to minister in his own strength, he fails to let God maximize the opportunity. A Christian should be "pumped up" for God, but his invigoration to serve in the name of Christ must not be obnoxious. When a believer loses his luster for God, he has begun quenching the Spirit that dwells within him (3:17).

But Paul prays that Christ might dwell in his readers' hearts. Since Paul was writing to Christians, does this phrase contradict the Scripture that says the Spirit of Christ already dwells within the hearts of believers (I Cor. 6:19)? No! The indwelling of Christ is a matter of degrees. It progressively reinforces divine security whereby one's faith is strengthened in proportion to the energy he expends in the performance of his salvation (Phil. 2:12). The Greek word translated "dwell" in verse 3:17 is *katoikeō*, which refers to permanent residence as a settler, and not temporary habitation as an alien. Paul prays that the Spirit of Christ will become permanently rooted in the hearts of believers in such a way that they know He controls their lives.

Love. Fourth, a mature Christian exhibits the abundance of love. Paul prayed for his readers to be "rooted and grounded in love" (3:17); so, too, believers today must become firmly entrenched in love so that others may know they are disciples of Christ (John 13:35). Love cannot be superficial. It has to be "rooted" as a tree and "grounded" as a building foundation. Both roots and foundations are unseen. Love often works behind the scenes; it does not boast or seek its own (I Cor. 13:4-5). Too many of us today profess love and flash a "Chesire cat" smile to fool people into believing that we are Mr. or Mrs. Love Plus. A mature Christian exudes love in serving others.

Congregationalism. Fifth, a mature Christian participates in a congregation. In 3:18, Paul prays that believers "be able to comprehend with all the saints what is the breadth and length and height and depth" of Christ's love. We should understand corporately that nothing can separate us from the love of Christ (Rom. 8:39). His love unifies all believers. Christians who isolate themselves will have a limited knowledge of God's love. They will not experience the power or the vibrancy of *agape* love. Isolation leads to hermitage, and hermits only serve themselves. Christians are called to be united in Christ to experience the fulness of God. A mature believer will be actively involved in the community of faith.

Education. Sixth, a vibrant believer knows "the love of Christ which surpasses knowledge" (3:19). Knowledge as the world understands it only makes one prideful and arrogant (I Cor. 8:1). Paul wants his readers to experience and understand the reality of Christ's love as well as the activity it promotes. A person grows in the knowledge of this love by obeying the commands of Christ, for Jesus said, "if you love me, keep my commandments" (John 14:15). Love is serving one another as Christ served and loved His church (5:2). His love had no limits but even went all the way to the cross for us.

We need education in Christ's love, for although we can never understand the breadth and length and height and depth of it (5:18), we must aspire to "be filled up to all the fulness of God" (5:19), be conformed to the image of Christ (Rom. 8:29). Paul's petition alludes to heavenly perfection. Although our sinful nature keeps us from this perfection, we must not forsake the challenge of emulating Christ and becoming perfect like Him. A mature Christian will continue to educate himself in Christ and the Word of God, for our heavenly Father expects us to grow daily toward the fulness that awaits us in Him. If we find ourselves not reading the Bible regularly and not getting involved with the study of Scripture, our maturity may be less than we believe it is. A Christian will not grow if he forsakes the study of God's Word. Just as we eat food for bodily growth, we need Scripture for our spiritual lives to thrive.

Spirit power. Seventh, a mature Christian recognizes the power of the Holy Spirit working within him (3:20). Too many times, we, as believers, fall back into our worldly attitudes and give ourselves credit for accomplishing difficult or challenging tasks. Pride emerges again as the dominant trait, and we relish the thought of self-achievement. Augustine called pride the foremost of sins, for it leads us away from God and into ourselves. The apostle John tells us that "the boastful pride of life" does not come from the Father, but rather emanates from the world (I John 2:16). A believer who has matured in Christ will sense when worldly pride wells up and defeat it immediately. He knows that pride leads to his own destruction (Prov. 16:18), and that to have reverence for the Lord is to hate pride and arrogance, which lead to evil (Prov. 8:13).

A Christian understands that everything he does, whether in word or deed, he does in the name of the Lord (Col. 3:17). Even in a boring or uncomfortable work situation, the believer must perform his duties for the Lord by doing the best job possible. He should not criticize or "slack off," but rather energetically accomplish his tasks in a commendable manner. When a circumstance appears intolerable, and a believer finds it difficult to perform for an unlikeable boss, that Christian ought to call upon the strength of God's Spirit within him to persevere and produce quality work. Although Christians may find this nearly impossible to do, Christ does not. All of us need to remember that we can do anything *through* Christ who strengthens us (Phil. 4:13), "for it is God who is at work in [us], both to will and to work for His good pleasure" (Phil. 2:13).

Recognizing the Spirit within us means acknowledging the third person of the Trinity. A professing Christian believes in the Godhead: Father, Son, and Holy Spirit—three persons in One.

Perpetuation of faith. Eighth, a mature Christian realizes his duty to perpetuate the faith among his family. As he gives glory to God "in the church and in Christ Jesus" (3:21), he tells of the Lord's work and glory "to all generations forever and ever" (3:21). The Christian's family comprises both the church (the body of Christ) and his own household. This is the new society about which Paul writes. In Christ, a new humanity has been re-created. As part of this humanity, the believer takes seriously his call to speak and to live the gospel he propagates. He begins with his own household, for if his household is not in order, he will not be able to care for the body of Christ (I Tim. 3:5).

Paul admonishes the believer to rear his children "in the discipline and instruction of the Lord" (6:4). God commissions the father as spiritual head of the household and holds him accountable for the raising of the children. God through Moses commanded us to teach His words diligently to our children and to talk about his ways constantly (Deut. 6:7). A believer builds a chain and constructs links between the church, home, and school. If one area is weak, the chain will snap. If we have no regular devotions or discussions about the Lord at home, we should not be surprised if our children rebel against our lifestyles. The greatest amount of instruction should take place in the home. Sunday school will not make spiritual giants of our children; rather, their spirituality will develop in proportion to the amount of love and teaching that comes from their parents. The hours children today spend under the influence of peers and the school system make parental instruction even more important. Parents who have children in public schools must work doubly hard to foster the faith with which God has sovereignly blessed them.

If our homes are in order and each link of the chain solid, then the curse in Exodus 20:5 will be averted. The iniquity of our fathers and ourselves will not be visited upon our children to the third and fourth generations. As strong believers, we realize the need to cease sinning, if not for our own well-being, then at least for the benefit of our posterity. God is a jealous God, says Scripture. He will not tolerate our putting any idols before Him. If we become lethargic in disciplining our children and in personally teaching them the ways of the Lord, we put ourselves and our own apathy on the throne of our lives. In other words, we become our own idols, for we have relegated God to a secondary position. In such a case, we may experience God's wrath through various circumstances including rebellion in our children, for our sins will be visited upon them, that is, they will experience the consequences of our misdeeds.

Application of Ephesians 3:14-21

1. I want to have a love relationship with Christ. To enhance this relationship I will _____

   _____ (do something).

   Applied: Yes _____   No _____

2. Paul prayed that believers would become more Christ-like by showing humility, by being identified with God's household, by ministering to others with vigor, by displaying love, by becoming more involved with the local congregation of believers, by seeking more teaching in the Word of God, by recognizing that the Holy Spirit works within and through them, and by perpetuating the faith through family instruction and training. I know I am

deficient in one or more of the above, especially _____

_____

(list where deficient).

I will work at becoming more mature by endeavoring to _____

_____

(what you will do to clear up deficiencies).

                              Applied: Yes _____ No _____

Questions for Ephesians 4:1-16

1. Paul specifies five qualities that should characterize a Christian's
   walk. What are they (4:2-3)?

   a.

   b.

   c.

   d.

   e.

2. What does Paul mean by one baptism (4:5)?

3. What does it mean that Christ descended into the lower part of the earth (4:9)? See Psalm 16:10 and Acts 2:24-28.

4. How can we stop from being children tossed about by winds of doctrine (4:14-16)?

8

Unity in the Body of Christ

Transition (4:1-3)

Paul begins this section of Scripture with the word "therefore" to make the transition from doctrine to practice. Having instructed the Gentiles in the hope of their calling (1:18), he now shifts to how their behavior should reflect this calling. "I . . . entreat you to walk in a manner worthy of the calling" (4:1).

His prayer (3:14-21) just previous to this section gave his readers an indication of what a mature Christian should demonstrate. Paul now encourages his readers to walk in a manner leading to this maturity in terms of five qualities. First, a Christian's walk should evidence humility (4:2), a word the Greeks never used in the context of admiration. To the Greek mind, *tapeinotes* (lowliness) meant a servile attitude no better than the submissiveness displayed by a cowering slave. The word Paul uses in 4:2 for humility is *tapeinophrosunē*, "lowliness of mind." Christ had this mind when He lowered Himself as a bond servant in order to submit Himself unto death (Phil. 2:7-8) and became a curse for an adulterous and undeserving people. Christ voluntarily chose to be a servant (Matt. 20:28) who humbled Himself before the mighty hand of God (I Pet. 5:6) for the benefit of His elect (1:4-5). Can we not lower our minds by putting aside our pride? We are called to be servants, for this fosters unity in the body of Christ.

Second, a Christian is gentle. If one has the humility of mind to subject himself to another (5:21), his demeanor will illustrate gentleness (4:2). In the Greek, the word is *praotēs*, sometimes translated "meekness." Jesus said, "Blessed are the meek [gentle], for they shall inherit the earth" (Matt. 5:5). How do the meek inherit the temporal earth? Many people equate meekness with a certain "mouseyness" or weakness. On the contrary, the word denotes silent, personal strength. A person who displays this meekness actively involves himself in service to others and never asserts his rights to someone else's detriment.

Third, a humble and gentle Christian displays patience (4:2). A person who does not display gentleness will surely show a lack of patience. As humility and gentleness go hand in hand, so, too, do gentleness and patience. Paul desires that his readers be long-suffering toward others and toward the circumstances in which they find themselves. A gentle person has little regard for his own personal claims or status. This quality of putting others first will necessarily lead to uncomplaining endurance of intolerable situations and people. If we have problems with our own patience, we should begin working on becoming more gentle.

Fourth, a Christian strives for forbearance (4:2), which naturally flows out of patience. Without patience, people cannot forbear one another, for to do so is a choice of mutual tolerance. To be tolerant of another means to indulge another's views and allow peace to permeate the body of Christ.

Fifth, a Christian diligently preserves the unity of the Spirit (4:3). If believers are not forbearing toward one another, they will not be diligent in preserving the peace. Diligence means careful, persistent effort applied to one's work or duty. Believers have the duty to preserve the unity of the body, but not at the expense of purity. Yet, if the believer prayerfully seeks each quality, both unity and purity will result, for each quality or trait includes interaction with people. If each believer practices humility, gentleness, patience, long-suffering, and diligence, each will portray a life worthy of his calling, the calling to be members in the one body, Christ Jesus.

Sevenfold Uniqueness (4:4-6)

Paul here uses the word "one" as an adjective seven times (4:4-6). Oneness is the goal of Christianity, for Christ prayed that His followers would be one as He and the Father are One (John 17:21), so

that believers might be perfected in unity (John 17:23). Paul emphasizes that there is one body for the precise reason that there is only
one Spirit (4:4) who has brought Jew and Gentile together as a new
humanity (2:14-16). This Spirit is the Spirit of Christ who is the
object of our one faith (4:5), in whom we are once and for all baptized
(4:5), and who represents the one and only hope (4:4) of our calling.
As believers, we have exercised faith in Christ in whom we are
identified through baptism, and we excitedly await His second
coming, knowing that without Christ we would be dead in our
trespasses and sins (2:1) and without hope. The second coming,
however, holds anxiety and dread for those who are unsaved and
have no hope of eternal bliss.

The household of God has assurance of heavenly reward, because
there is one God and Father whose sovereignty rules over and
penetrates all things (4:6). The all of whom God is Father (4:6) refers
to Christians, the household of faith (2:19) and not to all people in a
universal sense. (See the discussion of 1:5-8, under the heading of
"Adoption.") Since there is only one God, the Father, there is only
one household of faith, one family. This family is the invisible
church, which comprises all the saints from all time, and its members are known only to God. This church can never be severed, since
the Holy Spirit created her unity in the bond of peace (4:3).

The visible church, however, consists of many different groups or
denominations, which gives the world the impression that the church
is split. A number of varying convictions lead to denominationalism,
but the true believer, no matter his affiliation, is bonded with other
believers because Christ is the glue. The visible church does consist
of nonbelievers. Many pew sitters are only Sunday church goers
and have no heart for the Lord. Whenever a group of "on-fire
Christians" belong to the same church as "sedentary world-
watchers," tension and conflict inevitably result. Peace in the local
body can be secured only when Christ, not self, becomes the object
of each member's devotion.

One Baptism (4:5)

The true believer needs only one baptism (4:5), not two or more.

Some groups have taught much about two baptisms—water and Spirit. Baptism comes from the Greek word *baptizō*, "to be identified with." A cloth or garment placed into a dye was said to be identified with a new color when it was pulled out. We have one baptism conferred upon us by God the Father, which identifies us with God the Son. Being born of the Spirit, therefore, is the work of God. We have nothing to do with it. Baptism by water is the outward and visible sign by which we become publicly identified with the household of God. *It is not* the instrument of salvation. It is merely a sign of entrance into the visible church. In Acts 10:48, Peter commanded the new converts from the house of Cornelius to be "baptized in the name of Jesus Christ." The Spirit had come upon these Gentiles by God's choice. Peter, therefore, ordered water baptism as an expression of their identification with Jesus Christ.

The Trinity Mentioned (4:4-6)

The Trinity was an integral part of Paul's emphasis on oneness and unity. God the Holy Spirit (4:4), God the Son (4:5), and God the Father (4:6) are not three separate entities, but one God existing in three persons with different functions to perform. The Trinity can be likened to the sun, which is one entity, yet it exists with three noticeable facets: all separate, all different, yet all are one.* The fiery ball represents the mass of the star around which planets rotate. In this sense the sun is the center of the solar system as God the Father is the basis for all life. Yet, the sun also provides light, the rays of which can be seen as proceeding from the center although they are in substance the sun itself. Jesus as God the Son proceeded from the Father and became light to all the nations (John 8:12). Originating from the center and from the emanating rays of the sun is the energy

*There is no perfect illustration for a paradox such as the Trinity. Attempting to illustrate the Trinity subjects one to charges of heresy because there really is no adequate illustration for the Triune God. Even the "sun" illustration appears to be modalistic. But God does not merely manifest Himself in three ways. He is, at the same time, God the Father, God the Son, and God the Holy Spirit. If we say that God only shows Himself in one of the three ways, we imply that God does not exist as three distinct persons, and that He merely manifests distinct characteristics in order to perform different functions.

of heat. Although we can't see the warmth, we can feel it and know that it exists as the sun exists, for the sun is heat. Although the Holy Spirit cannot be seen, His presence and equality with God are sensed and known, and like heat proceeding from the sun, the Spirit proceeds from the Father (John 15:26).

When critics say the term "Trinity" does not appear in the Bible and is, therefore, unscriptural, they have failed to investigate the importance of this doctrine to the apostles. Though formulations of the doctrine are post-apostolic, the Trinity, nonetheless, was thoroughly apostolic in origin. Here in Ephesians we see the importance of Paul's three-in-one concept. The word "Trinity" does not appear, but the concept and word formulations do. In Titus 3:4-6, we again see the formulation of the Trinity: Paul calls God "our Savior" (v. 4), who saved us through regeneration by the Holy Spirit (v. 5), who was given to us through the atoning act of Jesus Christ our Savior (v. 6). Notice that God the Father equals our Savior in verse 4, and Jesus Christ equals our Savior in verse 6. Therefore, God the Father and Christ the Son are equal in substance in the minds of the apostles. Verse 5 tells us that God's Holy Spirit was "poured out upon us richly through Jesus Christ," again, connecting the three persons—God the *Father* whose *Spirit* regenerated the elect through the work of God the *Son*. Clearly, the apostles emphasized and taught the doctrine of the Trinity.

The Gift of Christ (4:7-8)

Paul shifts from unity to diversity in 4:7. He changes his words from "all" in 4:6 to "each" in 4:7 to emphasize the individual. Although we are unified in the body of Christ, we are not mere humanoids or exact replicas of each other. We are different because God has created us uniquely and because Christ has bestowed various gifts upon us. The measure of grace given is proportionate to the specific gift or gifts bestowed on a believer. Each should freely receive his gift from the Lord and use it to accomplish the functions and duties the gift represents.

Paul sees the bestowing of gifts as fulfilling Psalm 68:18 (4:8), which the Jews repeated in synagogue worship on the day of Pentecost. The psalm refers to a king who victoriously ascends on high (4:8) with a procession of captives. This indicated that the king had taken tribute and distributed it among his subjects. Paul sees Christ as the ascending king who led men from the captivity of hell and bestowed upon them gifts to serve Him in His new kingdom.

The Lower Parts of the Earth (4:9-10)

The same king who ascended had first "descended into the lower parts of the earth" (4:9). What does this mean? Calvin thought the phrase meant that Christ had first descended to earth in order to accomplish the task of redemption. Having thus secured salvation for the elect, He then ascended on high to sit at the right hand of the Father.

Other commentators believe that Christ descended into the lower regions of the earth, that is, Hades or Sheol. Hades was the abode of the dead; David prayed that his soul not be abandoned to this place (Ps. 16:10). In the same verse, David said that the Holy One would not undergo decay in Sheol (Ps. 16:10). Acts 2:25-28 quotes David and indicates that at death Christ descended into Hades, but the power of hell could not hold him (Acts 2:24). Christ was, therefore, resurrected and "ascended far above all the heavens" (4:10), where He was exalted by the Father to sit at His right hand (Ps. 110:1).

Offices Bestowed (4:11-13)

Christ was exalted to the Father's right hand in order to fill all things (1:23; 4:10). In other words, the Spirit of Christ pervades the entire universe; thus, all believers can experience His presence at the same time. "Lo, I am with you always, even to the end of the age" (Matt. 28:20).

Since the Spirit of Christ is everywhere, Christ commissions certain people to perform various functions within the body. "And He gave some as apostles, and some as prophets, and some as evangelists, and some as pastors and teachers" (4:11). What purpose do these special ministries have? "The equipping of the saints

.or the work of service, to the building up of the body of Christ" (4:12). What is the reason for building and edifying? So that every believer can attain "unity of the faith" and have "the knowledge of the Son of God" in order to become a "mature man" of God (4:13).

Winds of Doctrine (4:14-16)

As a result of maturing in Christ, believers are no longer "children, tossed here and there by waves, and carried about by every wind of doctrine, by the trickery of men, by craftiness in deceitful scheming" (4:14). Paul prayed for the qualities of a mature believer to become evident in the lives of his readers and hearers (3:14-21). He entreated the saints to walk in a prescribed manner worthy of their calling (4:1-3). Paul desired that his readers become stable in the faith, which would prevent them from running after each new religious fad. Peter echoed the same sentiments and warned his readers to beware of false prophets and teachers "who will secretly introduce destructive heresies, even denying the Master who bought them, bringing swift destruction upon themselves" (II Pet. 2:1). Almost every epistle has a warning about false teaching. The only way to be assured of not unknowingly falling under the influence of subtle but destructive teaching is to become strong in the faith by living the Scriptures.

Being doers of the Word and not merely hearers (James 1:22) will result in speaking the "truth in love" and growing "in all aspects into . . . Christ" (4:15). In Christ all believers fit together in the body and are "held together by that which every joint supplies" (4:16). The believer may be likened to part of a puzzle. If a piece is missing, the puzzle is not complete. Each piece, however, fits perfectly together and has a specific place in relation to the whole. As part of the body of Christ, the individual believer has a specific "working" function—to respond to the head (Christ), causing "growth of the body for the building up of itself in love" (4:16).

Application of Ephesians 4:1-16

1. I realize that I have trouble with (check one) humility _____, gentleness _____, patience _____, forbearance _____, diligence _____.

   I will _____
   in order to overcome this fault to the glory of God.

                      Applied: Yes _____ No _____

2. I am identified with Christ and display my identification to my neighbors by _____.
   I suddenly realize I do not display the badge of Christ. I will, therefore, (do) _____
   _____ for my neighbor and give God the glory.

                      Applied: Yes _____ No _____

Questions for Ephesians 4:17-32

1. What do you suppose Paul meant by "Gentiles walking in the futility of their minds" (4:17)? See Romans 1:21-23.

2. How can we renew the spirit of our minds (4:23)? See Romans 12:2.

   a. (4:25)

   b. (4:26)

   c. (4:28)

   d. (4:29)

3. In 4:30 Paul says that the Holy Spirit has sealed us for the day of redemption. Yet in 1:7, he says we have already been redeemed. Is this an inconsistency? If not, how do you explain the difference?

   a.

   b.

4. Is forgiving another hard to do (4:32)? How do you go about forgiving another? List steps if necessary.

   a.

   b.

9

From Rags to Riches

———————— 4:17-32 ————————

The Gentile Walk (4:17-19)

Paul reiterates his entreaty in 4:1 that his readers walk "in a manner worthy of [their] calling": "This I say therefore, and affirm together with the Lord, that you walk no longer just as the Gentiles also walk" (4:17). Although Paul is writing to Gentile believers, he admonishes them not to walk as Gentiles. Paul means to contrast the old way with the new; since those in Christ are no longer labelled as either Jew or Gentile, Paul means that his readers should not do what pagans would do.

Just how do the pagans (Gentiles) walk? The Gentiles walk "in the futility of their mind" (4:17). The knowledge they pridefully claim is nothing more than folly, for they fool themselves into thinking they are wise (Rom. 1:22). Actually, they have become vain in their reasoning, not realizing that their understanding has become darkened (4:18). Paul says it is due to the "hardness of their heart" (4:18). The Greek word for hardness is *pōrōsis*, from the verb *pōroō*, to petrify or become hard. In this context the word refers to the willful "dulling of the mind." The Gentiles stubbornly seal their minds against God and do not honor Him as God (Rom. 1:21). As a result, they become ignorant within themselves and, therefore, are excluded from the life of God (4:18).

After their minds become "empty" to the truth of God, they become "callous" and insensitive to God's way of life. This careless indifference leads to a life of sensuality and impurity to such an extent that they crave it with greedy appetites (4:19). The more they crave, the more callous they become. And they become like callous skin that has lost its sensitivity. Although they were created and intended to live a life of moral order and example, in their callousness they can no longer differentiate between right and wrong. Instead they rationalize everything in their minds, to appease their own immoral appetites. Although the heathen choose this immoral lifestyle, God exercises His wrath upon them by giving them up to the lusts of their hearts (Rom. 1:24).

The Christian Walk (4:20-29)

But Paul's readers "did not learn Christ in this way" (4:20). No, they had "heard Him and [had] been taught in Him, just as truth is in Jesus" (4:21). They knew their "former manner of life" from which they had repented, having laid it aside (4:22). So then, Paul's readers should have understood the precepts and commands of Christ and sought to be renewed in the spirit of their minds (4:23). But how would they do this? By putting on a "new self which in the likeness of God has been created in righteousness and holiness of the truth" (4:24). God commands each believer to emulate Christ by clothing himself in righteousness and setting himself apart for the work Christ would have him do. Believers should not conform to the world's standards (Rom. 12:2), but rather empty themselves of the garbage the world heaps upon them.

Paul gives clear and concrete examples. First, lay aside falsehood and speak truth to each other (4:25). Be honest with other believers. Deceit does not come from the God of truth. Speaking falsely allows the father of lies (John 8:44) to enter and spread gossip. Paul quotes God's words through the prophet Zechariah (Zech. 8:16), who charged the people of Israel to speak and judge in truth so that peace would abound within the community. Thus, Paul refers here to peace among believers. To combat the spirit of divisiveness in the community, believers must become vulnerable, willing to "open up" to each other, and speak the truth in love.

Second, do not sin in anger (4:26). Again Paul turns to an Old Testament passage (Ps. 4:4) as an example of "renewing our minds." It is not sinful to be angry, Paul tells us. Why? Anger is an emotion, and we are created with emotions. Therefore, in and of themselves, emotions are good. When these emotions are misused, perverted, or abused, they become sinful. Paul recognizes the emotion of anger and warns us not to sin in our anger. The worldly way of handling anger is to lose control and become rageful or vengeful. Letting anger run to this excess would be sinful. Christ especially warned us not to be angry with our brother, for if we are, we are guilty before the court (Matt. 5:22).

In our relationships with one another, we must not let the sun go down on our anger (4:26). Paul instructs us to resolve our differences before we retire for the night. If we have not done so, then the seeds of discontent, rejection, jealousy, and so forth will fester within us, and in the morning we will wake with greater tension and conflict. This is why Psalm 4:4 says, "Meditate in your heart upon your bed and be still." God wants us to relax at the close of the day. We should release all the tension that has built up and be free to commune with God.

By not facing a problem we have with another person, we let the sun go down on our wrath. In so doing we give the devil a foothold in our lives (4:27). When we nurse our wrath or bitterness against others, we invite the great adversary to exploit our indignation. In such a situation we fall further away from the righteousness God expects of us (James 1:20).

Third, avoid thievery (4:28). "Do not steal" is the eighth commandment passed down to us through Moses. It means more than not pilfering money or possessions. In today's society, stealing includes tax evasion, taking advantage of laborers, mistreating business associates, and not giving 100 percent of our working effort to our employers. It is not enough to stop stealing; one must start working with his own hands to earn a decent wage. The reformed thief ought thereby to share with others in need (4:28).

Fourth, maintain a decent tongue. Paul admonishes his readers, "Let no unwholesome word proceed from your mouth" (4:29). With a renewed mind, we are to speak appropriate words that edify (4:29). Words have great significance, for they reveal what our hearts contain (Matt. 12:34). Jesus says we will give an account of every careless word we have uttered (Matt.12:36). If we are new creatures in Christ, our language and communication will encourage and comfort people in time of need. Our "gutter language" should disappear, for no longer should our tongues be a raging fire that defiles and consumes the whole body (James 3:6).

Grieving the Holy Spirit (4:30)

Paul shifts from warning us against vile language to commanding us not to "grieve the Holy Spirit by whom [we] were sealed for the day of redemption" (4:30). Three verses prior to this one Paul recognized the devil as a personal being. Now he acknowledges the Holy Spirit as fully personal. We know this by the Greek word he used for "grieve." *Lupeō* means to cause pain, sorrow, or distress, and only persons can feel such things. But how does one grieve the Holy Spirit? Since the Spirit is holy, pure, and righteous, He would be grieved by the practice of unrighteousness. Since He is also "one Spirit" (4:4), He would be grieved by disunity among the body of believers. Anything incompatible with purity and unity within the church would grieve the Spirit.

Paul tells his readers the Spirit has sealed them for the day of redemption. At first glance, this statement appears inconsistent with Paul's previous statement in 1:7, in which he tells us we already have redemption through the blood of Christ. Paul means in 4:30 that we have already been sealed with the Spirit of Christ (which occurred at the moment of rebirth), but now we await the day when our bodies will be completely redeemed (which indicates true liberation). "Sealing" refers to the beginning of our Christian walk and "redemption" looks toward its culmination at the second coming, when the sons of God are revealed (Rom. 8:19).

Paul's Summation (4:31-32)

Paul sums up what it takes to have a renewed mind and what to avoid in order not to grieve the Holy Spirit. "Let all bitterness and wrath and anger and clamor and slander be put away from you, along with all malice (4:31). If a believer sets aside these vices, which cause disharmony, unity among the community of faith results. Yet, a believer should realize that he is in a spiritual battle, and his enemy who seeks to devour him will continue to exploit these annoyances to the detriment of the community. A Christian must learn to resist these demonic but subtle strategies, for the Evil One will employ the same tactics until he realizes that his target (us) has overcome these temptations and is no longer influenced by them. Then the devil will flee from us (James 4:7) and desist from such annoyances.

Bitterness is a spirit gone sour, a spirit that refuses to reconcile. It is an acid that eats the container from inside out. The person holding the resentment lets it eat at him until it harms both him and his relationships with others. God created us as relational beings, and He admonishes us to heal embittered relationships. Refusal to do so allows the acid to eat away at our lives and our witness for Christ.

Wrath and anger are closely associated. Wrath denotes rage to the point of vengeance, whereas anger is more a controlled and darkened hostility. Anger, if not held in check, may fester into vindictiveness toward another and eventually lead to wrath. Clamor describes people who lose control during arguments and raise their voices or scream obscenities. Slander, on the other hand, is speaking evil against another and spreading lies to harm his reputation. Malice is premeditated ill will toward another. It involves actually plotting to harm someone physically or ruin his reputation.

All these vices have no place in the Christian community. To the contrary, Paul commands those within the community of faith to "be kind to one another, tender-hearted, forgiving each other, just as God in Christ also has forgiven [them]" (4:32). A Christian's life should evidence kindness, compassion, and forgiveness—the same qualities Christ demonstrated. We should practice them not only within the community of faith, but also within the world. We must love our enemies and show them kindness, expecting nothing in return (Luke 6:35). A believer will find this most difficult to do if he harbors bitterness and anger toward anyone, whether a believer or not. If we are bitter or angry toward anyone, we certainly will not be compassionate toward that person. A forgiving spirit begins here.

God forgave us through the atoning work of Christ. This in itself gives us incentive to forgive those who sin or trespass against us. If we do not forgive those who have caused us hurt, God will not forgive us (Matt. 6:15). How many times must we forgive? "Seventy times seven" (Matt. 18:22)—in other words, an indefinite number. The Greek word Paul uses here is *charizomai*, which has richer meaning than *aphiēmi*, the most common verb used for offering forgiveness. *Aphiēmi* denotes "letting go" or "letting off." Forgiveness in this sense means allowing a mistake or trespass against us and casting out of any bitterness within us. *Charizomai* goes a step further and primarily means "to bestow as a free gift." Though we may have cause to be angry and embittered, we must put away this right and give of ourselves as a free gift to one who is undeserving of our friendship. *Aphiēmi* might lead a believer to say, "Yeh, I forgive him," without any corresponding action to demonstrate this forgiveness. *Charizomai* tells us that we must make a sincere effort to confront those who sin against us, to relay our heart-felt intent to forgive them, and to offer ourselves back into a relationship with them. Forgiveness is not just saying the words; rather, it actively seeks a relationship with those who may be undeserving of our interaction.

Application of Ephesians 4:17-32

1. I really have _____/have not _____ (check one) been trying to walk "in a manner worthy of my calling" since this study began. I do not want to become as nonbelievers who Scripture says walk "in the futility of their minds." I want to become more involved in the body of Christ in order to think and act as a co-heir to the kingdom of God. I will become more involved in the local church by_____

   _____

   (your part in the functioning of the church).

   Applied: Yes _____   No _____

2. Grieving the Holy Spirit would include fostering disunity among the body of Christ. I have held bitterness against _____ _____ (a brother or sister in Christ).

   I will ask this person for forgiveness and seek to build or rebuild our relationship.

Applied: Yes _____   No _____

Questions for Ephesians 5:1-21

1. How does Paul say we ought to imitate God (5:1)?

    a. (5:2)

    b. (5:3)

    c. (5:4)

    d. (5:6)

    e. (5:11)

2. How does Paul say we walk as wise men (5:15)?

    a. (5:16)

b. (5:17)

c. (5:18)

d. (5:19)

e. (5:20)

f. (5:21)

3. Paul says, "Be subject to one another" (5:21). What does subjec-
   tion mean to you? How do you propose to subject yourself to
   another believer besides your spouse?

   a.

   b.

10

Be Imitators of God

Imitate Love (5:1-2)

Paul tells us to "be imitators of God, as beloved children" (5:1). This instruction immediately follows the injunction to forgive one another (4:32), for just as God forgives us, we should forgive others. In order to forgive others, a believer must "walk in love." Paul is speaking about the love that serves others, just as Christ demonstrated in offering Himself as a sacrifice on our behalf (5:2). Love is, first of all, an action. It is behavior that emanates in patience and kindness and is not arrogant or unbecoming. Love bears and endures all things, for it never fails (I Cor. 13:4-8).

Shed Your Old Clothes (5:3-5)

Paul turns from describing the service of love, which is the sacrifice of self, to exposing the indulgence of self. "Do not let immorality or any impurity or greed even be named among you" (5:3), and you will also imitate God. The opposite of love is lust, a sin that seeks to satisfy its own sexual appetites. The Greek word Paul uses for immorality is *porneia* and for impurity *akatharsia*. These two words cover every kind of sexual sin, from the lust of the mind to extra-(outside of) marital intercourse. To emphasize the seriousness of sexual sins, Paul adds the word "greed," also used in 4:19 to describe a type of impurity. In this context Paul refers to coveting someone's body in order to satisfy one's lust.

Paul continues his admonishment by telling his readers there should be "no filthiness and silly talk, or coarse jesting, which are not fitting" (5:4) among believers. Here, Paul instructs his readers to shed vulgarity as well as a dirty mind. In lieu of such obscenities, believers are to give thanks, for thankfulness recognizes God's gift of sex. Joking about it degrades the gift to the point of worthlessness.

Why is it important to have a clean mind and a decent mouth? Verse 5 answers this question: "No immoral or impure person or covetous man, who is an idolater, has an inheritance in the kingdom of Christ and God." Only those who are born again will enter the kingdom, and those who practice acts of immorality demonstrate a heart of stone. Ungodly practices point to an unregenerate heart, and unregenerate hearts do not inherit the kingdom of God. Worshiping their appetites, the unregenerate covet worldly things. They become idolaters, for their mind is set on lust or materialism and not on the things of God.

Beware of Deception (5:6-8)

After putting away the old self, which focuses on immoral things, Paul issues a warning: "Let no one deceive you with empty words, for because of these things the wrath of God comes upon the sons of disobedience" (5:6). Since Paul has just admonished his readers to abstain from immorality, many commentators believe that Paul is issuing a caveat against a sect of Gnosticism that taught that immorality affected only the physical being and not the spiritual: since the body is not immortal, anything a person does with it is irrelevant to his spiritual well-being. Paul warns his readers to be on guard against this false teaching and not become partakers in it (5:7). In this way, also, you imitate God, for a believer has no cause to fall prey to deceptive teachings and false philosophies. He now walks as a child of the Light, who is Christ Jesus (5:8). He is no longer in darkness, for darkness and light cannot dwell together.

The Light Shines (5:9-14)

Paul tells us that if we do carry the candle of the Lord, our actions will consist "in all goodness and righteousness and truth" (5:9), and we will strive to please the Lord (5:10). Since Christians have been taken out of the domain of darkness (Col. 1:13), they now have a responsibility to allow the light of Christ in them to shine forth in the world. In order to do this, they must "not participate in the unfruitful deeds of darkness, but instead even expose them" (5:11). There is no benefit in living in darkness, for the fruit of a godly life cannot ripen without light. In order for the maturation process to occur, a light source is needed. And when light is produced, darkness dissipates.

Christians, as imitators of God, are called to dissipate the darkness by exposing evil about them. Believers must put on their spiritual armor and fight the forces of evil. "Expose" is an active verb; Christians do not sit idly by and watch as evil spreads, but rather, they unmask evil and show it for what it is. Darkness must be exposed "for it is disgraceful even to speak of the things which are done by them in secret" (5:12).

Paul elaborates further in verse 13: "All things become visible when they are exposed by the light, for everything that becomes visible is light." Darkness camouflages the evil within the world. The light flushes evil out and exposes its ugly reality. But if a Christian refuses to be used as God's vessel to shine the light of Christ, evil will remain hidden in the darkness. Yet, if a Christian chooses to be God's spotlight, even the darkness may become light. In other words, God may very well use a believer as His instrument to bring a person out of the realm of darkness to experience the joy of eternal light. This is conversion—awaking from sleep and arising from the dead because Christ chose to shine His light on us (5:14).

Wisdom of a Lifestyle (5:15-21)

In order to imitate their beloved Father, believers must watch carefully how they walk. They must exhibit the lifestyles of wise men (5:15) by conducting themselves with wisdom toward those who are outside the faith and making the most of every opportunity (Col. 4:5). But how does one's lifestyle demonstrate the wisdom of knowing Christ?

First, a Christian makes the most of the time given him because the days are evil (5:16). Paul's era was filled with persecution and distress. People were conscious of how little time they had to work for the Lord. They took every opportunity to spread the good news. What about us? We live in a country that protects our freedoms. We do not need to suffer for the sake of Christ. Time does not seem urgent. Yet, the word Paul uses for "time" is *kairos*, which denotes a special or critical epoch or time frame. Paul is also writing for us today, saying: Make the most of each specific opportunity. Redeem your time. Get something out of the moments at hand, and do not let a chance to share the gospel slip through your fingers.

Second, a wise Christian learns the Lord's will (5:17). Knowing the Lord's desires for us is not a simple task. If we are out of fellowship with the Lord and avoid reading Scripture, we will never discern His will. He reveals His will through His Word and through godly counsel based on His Word. If we have no desire to go to His Word, we really have no desire to know His will. We will base our decisions upon what appeases our appetites or intellects and never apply the test of God's wisdom found in James 3:17.

Third, a wise Christian does not get drunk (5:18). Dissipation through alcoholic beverages is one of "the deeds of the flesh" (Gal. 5:21) that may exclude a person from the kingdom of heaven (I Cor. 6:10). A Christian who abuses alcohol is a poor witness for Christ. The beverage itself is not the sin, but its misuse, abuse, or perversion is sinful. However, if a believer knows that strong drink presents a stumbling block to another, he should not cause his brother or family member to stumble by indulging. Rather, he should be filled with the Spirit (5:18). This is not to say we become inebriated with the Spirit of Christ so that we lose control of our faculties. It is just the opposite, for being in the Spirit means we have self-control, the last fruit of the Spirit (Gal. 5:23).

We find the marks of spiritual fulness in 5:19-21. These same marks are three additional indicia for walking in wisdom. First, Paul says, we should speak to one another in psalms and hymns and spiritual songs and sing and make melody with our hearts to the Lord (5:19). In order to speak to one another, we must be in fellowship with each other. A wise Christian does not forsake the assembling together. Paul seems to have in view a worship setting where believers not only sing to the Lord but also exhort each other to sing praises. Psalms may refer to the Old Testament psalter, hymns to Christian canticles, and spiritual songs to compositions that edify the body.

Some commentators believe that by spiritual songs, Paul means unpremeditated "vocaling" in the Spirit. The problem with this view is our inability to determine whether these melodic outpourings are in the Spirit and whether they are edifying to the body of believers. If the words are not discernable, one cannot establish whether they are of God or are enlightening to others.

We should not take the phrase "singing and making melody with your heart to the Lord" as being included in or connected with "speaking to one another in psalms and hymns and spiritual songs." The verbs "singing" and "making" seem to refer to both vocal and instrumental music that is directed to the Lord rather than to one another. This music doesn't necessarily have to be a psalm, a hymn, or a spiritual song. It is music that comes from the heart and may take a number of different forms.

Second, a Spirit-filled Christian is marked by the thanksgiving he offers for all things in the name of Christ (5:19). Paul frequently summons us to give thanks (Col. 3:15; I Thess. 5:18). We must not tolerate the murmuring spirit, for grumbling breeds discontent, and discontent affronts God by calling Him insufficient. To the contrary, we should give God thanks for what we have. Thankfulness signifies contentment. It recognizes the sovereignty of God who provides graciously all our needs.

Third, Spirit-filled Christians subject themselves to each other (5:21). Again, Paul stresses that the faithful humble themselves and mutually serve each other. The Greek word *hupotassomenoi* means to voluntarily submit. Submission is an exercise of the will in which a person chooses to become vulnerable, accountable, and surrendered to another. The Christian community should be a vibrant, pulsating, service organization in which people give of themselves without demanding anything in return.

Application of Ephesians 5:1-21

1. God wants us to shed our old clothes, which include immorality,

impurity, greed, obscenity, filthy mouths, coarse jesting, and heavy drinking. I do have a problem with _____ _____ (one or more of the above). I propose to _____ _____ (course of action to conquer this problem).

Applied: Yes _____   No _____

2. I understand that I carry the candle of the Lord, and His Light shines through me. I will not be fearful in living for Christ. I will pray that God will arrange the opportunity for me to share my faith with _____ (a nonbeliever) this week. I will not rationalize my fear by thinking I never had the opportunity or the time.

Applied: Yes _____   No _____

Questions for Ephesians 5:22-33

1. What does Paul call wives to do (5:22, 33)? How can this be accomplished?

    a.

    b.

2. How are husbands told to love their wives?

    a. (5:25)

b. (5:26)

c. (5:27)

d. (5:28)

3. In 5:31, what do you feel God meant by husband and wife becoming one flesh?

11

The Husband-Wife Relationship

The Christian Household

Paul has called us to submit to one another (5:21). What better place to put our servanthood into practice than in the home! The family household should exemplify God's new society. If the home is not strong and not functioning under the standards of God's new humanity, the church, which is composed of family units, will certainly not be the vibrant and active institution God has called it to be. Paul wants his readers to establish biblically strong intra-family relationships. This strength and scriptural soundness provides the basis for church and community involvement.

Paul also wanted his readers to be prepared for spiritual battle (6:12), for the greatest battleground exists in the home. Beginning with the fall of Adam and Eve, Satan took advantage of God's curse on the husband-wife relationship (Gen. 3:16), and Satan's strategy has not drastically changed. Throughout the history of mankind, Satan has been undermining the family structure, for the greatest single factor contributing to the fall of every major civilization has been the deterioration of the family unit. America has not escaped the battle! With first-time divorces occurring at a rate in excess of 50 percent, and second marriages ending in divorce at an alarming rate of approximately 70 percent, America is succumbing to the strategy of Satan.

Satan has also snared the Christian household, for it has not been immune to divorce. Christians have found it easier to appease themselves by fleeing distasteful marriages under the guise of "biblical divorce." Many believers have found it less painful to retreat from a God-approved relationship than to seek reconciliation. They have rationalized Malachi 2:16, in which God cries forth that He hates divorce. They have twisted God's concern about family deterioration by thinking that God primarily wants them to have peace within themselves. Yet God says, "There is a way which seems right to a man, but its end is the way of death" (Prov. 16:25).

The Tension in Marriage

In Genesis 3:16, God told Eve that her "desire shall be for her husband." The Hebrew word for desire is *tishuka,* which does not connote lust or even love toward her husband. The word derives from *shoq,* which means to run or have a violent craving. We find this same word in Genesis 4:7, where God warned Cain that sin crouched at the door of his heart and its desire (*shoq*) was for him. The "desire" is a hungering, lurching, and covetous craving. Not content with what it has, it will manipulate and seek to control in order to get its way. God said that Eve would now have a craving to control her husband. She would not be content with her subordination to the man. No longer would she (and women in general) naturally assume the role of helpmate to or counterpart of the man (Gen. 2:18). Originally created as a responder, a woman becomes a manipulator outside of Christ.

Although the wife seeks to control her husband, God says that "he shall rule over her." In this context, the Hebrew word *mashal* does not mean a kindly or benign rule. It connotes a domineering attitude. The man was first created to be an initiator, the one who would assume leadership responsibilities in the family and in the community. Because of the tension now placed upon marriages, a woman's manipulation will surface in her initiating various schemes to appease and satisfy her own selfish appetites. The man, in his unloving rule, will rebel against the woman's attempt at control by retreating from the situation. Or he will either give in to the persistent control techniques or wield his authority in a manner that drives him further away from his wife. The roles have been reversed; women in order to satisfy themselves have become initiators, and men in order to assert their rule have responded to the women's tactics of manipulation.

Submission and Authority (5:22-24)

Paul knew of God's curse on the marital relationship. He knew that for a husband and wife to experience the blessings of the God-ordained institution of marriage, they had to be rightly related to Christ. Therefore, Paul says, "Wives, be subject to your own husbands, as to the Lord" (5:22). The words "be subject" do not appear in the Greek manuscripts, but are supplied from the previous verse in which we are all to be subject to one another (5:21). However, in Paul's companion letter to the Colossians, the words "be subject" do appear, for Paul instructs wives to submit to their husbands "as is fitting in the Lord" (Col. 3:18). To be subjected to her husband, the wife must choose to do so; submission is voluntary. Obedience is demanded, but obedience itself is a choice. We can either choose to follow the Lord or choose to satisfy our own pleasures.

"Submission" in the Greek sense (*hupotassomai*) is a military word that refers to the ordering (*taxis*) of military rank. As a private is subjected to the authority of a sergeant or a colonel to the authority of a general, so too is a wife subjected to her husband. She is by no means inferior to her husband, nor is she to be lorded over by someone with a caveman mentality. The woman has been created in the image of God, for God created humanity, male and female (Gen. 1:27). Both the husband and the wife represent mankind. However, God did give each sex a certain office to hold and function to perform. In the military sense, the married woman is a colonel and the man the general. A general would never enter battle without seeking counsel from his colonels. Similarly, a husband should never make a major family decision without consulting his wife. After praying, meditating, and consulting with his wife, a husband must make the final decision. If that decision is contrary to biblical principles, the wife should not support or follow it, for Scripture commands a wife to submit "as fitting in the Lord" (Col. 3:18). Any request that violates the teachings of Christ, whether blatant or subtle, she must reject, for the woman lives foremost for Christ.

God's ordering of society and the family unit requires the wife's submission to her husband's authority. A husband stands in authority over his wife only because God has so ordained. The man exercises authority delegated to him. Therefore, when a wife subjects herself to her husband, she also subjects herself to God. If the husband violates, misuses, or abuses his God-given authority, a wife is no longer required to submit to him, for her first allegiance is to the Lord.

The husband is the head of the wife as Christ is the head of the church (5:23). Just as the church owes obedience to Christ, so, too, does the wife owe obedience to her husband. As Christ is Savior and Redeemer of the community of faith, so, too, is the husband the protector and deliverer of his wife. Paul emphasizes the importance of the wife's submission to her husband by analogizing her obedience to that required of the church in following Christ (5:24). Christ is the cornerstone of our faith. We as His body of believers can count on His sure foundation. We depend upon Him as the rock of our salvation and object of our faith. In similar fashion, the husband has been called to be the cornerstone within the family. He is the pressure bearer upon which his wife can confidently rely. If he abdicates his responsibility as the head and cornerstone of the family, the household foundation will totter and eventually crumble leaving the family unit in rubble.

Husbands to Love Wives (5:25-31)

Paul knew that a sure family foundation depended upon the strength of the cornerstone, the husband. He tells husbands to love their wives as Christ loved the church and gave Himself up for her (5:25). The wife submits to her husband; the husband has the corresponding duty to love her in a sacrificial way. This type of love is more than a natural or physical affection. It involves much more than emotionalism. Such love is active, not passive, has continual concern for a wife's well-being, and goes out of the way to protect the wife from indignation, insecurity, and a sense of worthlessness. Christ had a love of service, of giving of Himself. A husband's love should be no less, for he, too, should serve his wife in a sacrificial way and place satisfying her above satisfying himself.

Why did Christ give Himself for the church? First, to "sanctify her, having cleansed her by the washing of water with the word" (5:26). In sanctifying the church He set her apart for Himself. Before sanctification, however, Christ cleansed the church from sin and guilt through His sacrificial death and atonement. Baptism, which appears to be the reference of "washing of water," is the symbol of Christ's work of cleansing through the Holy Spirit. We should not take this phrase to mean that baptism is a salvatory rite. The additional reference "with the word" indicates that baptism as a sacrament needs to be accompanied by an explanatory word that defines the actual significance of the rite itself. The Greek word for "word" is *rhema*, which means spoken word rather than written word. This seems to corroborate the view that the word that expresses the promises of cleansing and rebirth must be vocalized during the baptism ceremony.

Some commentators believe that the spoken word is the baptismal candidate's profession of faith during the baptismal rite. They cite, as support, Romans 20:8ff., which says that we must confess with our mouth that Jesus is Lord. However, Paul was not talking about baptism when he penned this confession. He was referring to the time of regeneration or rebirth, which is the work of the Spirit. Furthermore, if this were the case, infant baptism, which was consistently practiced by the post-apostolic Christians, would have no covenantal validity or significance and would, therefore, be in contradiction to what Paul said in Colossians 2:11-12, where he made baptism an analogy of circumcision. Circumcision didn't mean an Israelite was saved. It only pointed to a covenantal relationship within the community of faith. Likewise, baptism points to this covenantal relationship and is extended to children of believers.

As Christ set apart the church for Himself, a husband sets apart his wife and holds her in high esteem. A husband's self-sacrificing love leads him to sanctify his wife by protecting her from ungodly influences and by speaking highly of her to others. He encourages and praises her as she seeks to minister to him.

Second, Christ gave of Himself to the church to present her "in all her glory, having no spot or wrinkle or any such thing; but that she should be holy and blameless" (5:27). The church could never have made herself beautiful or presentable to Christ, for all of our right-eousness is as filthy rags (Isa. 64:6). Beautifying the church was the labor of the Bridegroom, Christ. His labor perfected His bride and liberated her from the ugliness of sin. Likewise, a husband loves his wife by beautifying her through encouragement and praise before their children and others. He does not disfigure her physically or mentally, but promotes a sincere and holy reputation for her. He prevents contamination from seeping into their relationship and actively asserts his spiritual headship. God designated the husband as the spiritual umbrella that protects his family. If he allows his umbrella to be penetrated by shirking his spiritual responsibilities, sin and ungodliness will rain in on him and his family.

Paul returns specifically to the marital relationship in 5:28 and advises husbands "to love their own wives as their own bodies." Paul refutes the view that a wife is a slave or chattel of her husband. Rather, she should be considered an extension of the husband's personality, for God has called the two to become one flesh (5:31). A husband who treats his wife harshly as one may a slave has no regard for himself, for in mistreating his wife, he says to God that he also hates himself (5:29). A husband who has high regard for himself will nourish and cherish his wife as an extension of himself (5:30). This will produce peace and harmony within the family unit.

As the church receives her sustenance and security in the Lord (5:30-31), so too a wife receives her sustenance and security from her husband. A man who cares for his own body by feeding it, groom-ing it, and clothing it owes the same duty to his wife—to look after her health, comfort, and well-being.

Becoming one flesh not only signifies a sexual union, but also a union of personalities. Sexual intercourse should be an expression of deep love in which both husband and wife give of themselves. Sex is a gift from God, His stamp of approval on the bond of matrimony, for through this union of bodies God directs new lives to enter the world. Yet procreation is not the main purpose of sexual intercourse. Rather, the expression of mutual love and appreciation is the primary purpose. In the marriage bed husbands and wives can experience the blessed gift of mutual union that God ordained to bring man and wife closer together. Any sharing of bodies outside the marriage bed is an affront to God.

The Mystery of Union (5:32-33)

The mystery of becoming one is great (5:32), for the husband and wife become one in flesh and one in spirit. Through sexual intercourse two people become vulnerable and transparent to one another. Prior to the fall, Adam and Eve were naked but not ashamed (Gen. 2:25). Nakedness represented their innocence, openness, and vulnerability to each other. Sexual union involves both body oneness and spirit oneness. In the marriage bed the nakedness of husband and wife fosters spirit oneness because they share not only each other's bodies, but also each other's vulnerabilities.

Paul speaks about the mystery of union in "reference to Christ and the church" (5:32). Why God chose to elect some unto salvation to become part of His body is a mystery! Only God's Spirit knows the depths of God's mind (I Cor. 2:10). However, once members of God's body, we are always members. This speaks to the lifelong union of husband and wife. God warns husbands not to deal treacherously with the wives of their youth or to divorce them, for they have been given in marriage as companions through a covenant (Mal. 2:14-16).

Verse 33 sums up this section by reiterating that a husband must "love his own wife even as himself" and a wife must "respect her husband." For a wife to respect or revere her husband, a husband must give cause to be so respected. Yet even if a husband disobeys the Word, a wife must display chaste and respectful behavior, which may be the catalyst in winning her husband back into a relationship with her and more importantly with the Lord (I Pet. 3:1-2).

Application of Ephesians 5:22-33

1. I have not been ministering to my spouse (if married) or to my brother, sister, or friend (if not married). This week, in order to

serve him/her, I will _____
_____ (do something).

Applied: Yes _____   No _____

2. *Husbands:* I will love my wife as Christ loved the church by setting her apart in a special way. That way will be_____
_____
_____.

Applied: Yes _____   No _____

Wives: I will honor and respect my husband by _____
_____
_____ (doing something).

Applied: Yes _____   No _____

Singles: I will encourage _____
(a married friend) in his/her marriage by _____
_____ (action
or advice).

Applied: Yes _____   No _____

Questions for Ephesians 6:1-9

1. Disobedience to parents is a symptom of the disintegration of society (6:1). How do Romans 1:30 and II Timothy 3:2 support this view? Does honoring parents mean you must obey them as long as they live?

    a.

    b.

2. How might fathers provoke their children (6:4)? Why do you
   think Paul admonished fathers and not mothers?

   a.

   b.

3. Ephesians 6:5-9 concerns a servant-master or employee-
   employer relationship. What do you suppose Paul meant by
   "eye-service" (6:6)? What is a godly employment relationship
   (6:7-9)? Is Paul endorsing slavery? Why or why not?

   a.

   b.

   c.

12

Parent-Child and Master-Servant Relationships

_____ *6:1-9* _____

Disobedient Children (6:1-3)

Because God created us as relational beings, human relationships are very important. Paul previously exhorted Christian spouses (5:22-33) to practice their servanthood in Christ by ministering to one another. He now concentrates on parent-child and master-servant relationships. Paul had a family oriented view; he understood that disobedient children are symptomatic of social decay. A society that professes to know God, yet fails to honor Him as God (Rom. 1:21), will be riddled with foolishness. God turns a foolish society over to a depraved mind (Rom. 1:28) and lets the foolishness run its course, which eventually leads to the disintegration of that society (II Tim. 3:2). A society with libertarian views on raising children produces children who are rebellious and disobedient to their parents (Rom. 1:30). Therefore Christian parents must set the example by rearing a godly generation to check the tide of a decaying society.

"Children, obey your parents in the Lord" (6:1) is another of Paul's imperatives that display the submissiveness of one to another from verse 5:21. Paul specifically commands children to obey their parents and lists three reasons for doing so. First, it is the right thing to do (6:1). This speaks to the natural law God has written in the hearts of men and seared in the consciences of humankind (Rom. 2:15). Even a nonbeliever understands the importance of filial respect and the necessity of parental authority.

Second, God commanded, "Honor your father and mother" (6:2). But is honoring obeying? Honoring one's parents means acknowledging and accepting the authority God has given parents over children. Children recognize this delegated authority and realize that in honoring parents they obey God. To honor parents means to respect and revere them and includes the element of obedience. Reverence of parents was an integral part of the Hebrew society. Moses commanded the Israelites to revere and obey their parents; any stubborn and rebellious son who refused to obey his parents was put to death (Deut. 21:18-21).

Does honoring parents mean that a person must obey his parents as long as they live? Verse 1 commands children to obey their parents in the Lord. As long as a child remains under the roof of his father, he subjects himself to the authority of his parents. His father stands as God's delegated head of the family unit and, therefore, represents Christ to the whole family. A child receives the benefits of this representation and must obey his father and mother as God's ambassadors. A child's corporate identity in the Lord is familial.

As a child matures into adulthood and leaves the protection of the family unit, his identity becomes individualistic. He is no longer accountable directly to his parents for his lifestyle. He must answer to God, for the rod of chastisement will now come from his heavenly Father, not his earthly one. This does not mean he ceases to respect and revere his parents. On the contrary, he should still give great weight to their counsel. The final decision, however, rests with the emancipated son or daughter, for he or she is directly accountable to God, not to the parents.

Third, children who obey their parents receive a blessing: "That it may be well with you, and that you may live long on the earth" (6:3). This promise speaks to the stability of any society. Without a strong family unit, social stability crumbles. Does this mean that children must obey parents in everything? No! Only in the Lord (6:1). If a parent commands a child not to worship the Lord or not to follow Christ, the child must refuse to obey, for Christ must be our authority.

The Duty of Parents (6:4)

Paul shifts to parents and parental restraint of their authority:

"And fathers, do not provoke your children to anger; but bring them up in the discipline and instruction of the Lord" (6:4). Paul wishes fathers to be gentle, patient, persevering, and instructional.

A Roman father had sovereign authority. As head of his family, a Roman could kill his newborn or dispose of him as a slave. In other words, he could do anything he wanted, for he was a law unto himself.

Paul contrasts the Christian father with the pagan father. A believer has been given authority over his family by God and is not to abuse this authority by exasperating his children. A father should not make unreasonable demands upon his children or discipline in an arbitrary or unkind manner. This causes hostility and belligerence in children. A father should develop a child's potential, mold his personality in order to serve God, and encourage him in his gifts. He does this in a loving way and not in an oppressive authoritarian manner.

Children ask two questions in their family relationship. One, "Am I loved?" The other, "How much can I get away with?" Every nonconforming response should not be labeled "rebellion." Children will experiment with their liberty and in so doing test the quality of their parents' love. Boundaries, however, must be established. A child expects this and feels secure within the limits set. As he grows older, his parents extend the boundaries; but a child needs to know the extent of these boundaries and the consequences for stepping beyond them. Any parent who fails to deliver the consequences sends a message of "no love" to that child. A child expects discipline, for a loving parent will not spare the rod (Prov. 13:24). Although discipline will not seem joyful at the moment, it will yield the peaceful fruit of righteousness to those who have been trained by it (Heb. 12:11). As the Lord disciplines those whom He loves, parents likewise ought to discipline their children, for this displays love.

A father also has the responsibility to instruct his children in the Lord. The Greek word used is *nouthesia*, which could also be translated "warning." In any event, it refers to educating a child by word of mouth. This is not to say that education is indoctrination whereby a parent seeks to impose his or her mind and will on the child.

Ritualistic dogmatism produces boredom and restricts an inquisitive mind. Education is not forced compliance, but rather stimulation. The teacher presents stimuli and encourages the child to respond. This includes discussion and honest answering of questions. Parents use life's situations to convey God's truth. They take advantage of opportunities to teach God's way. This means *time*. Parents must spend many hours with their children, for without a quantity of time, there will be no quality. Quality time and lasting relationships will not occur without much effort, and effort takes time.

Slaves and Employees (6:5-8)

Paul turns from familial relationships to employment relationships. The stability of the family unit is a high priority. Yet, within each unit are people who have an employment relationship with someone else. If this relationship is not good, a disgruntled worker may carry his or her problems home, causing family tensions. Paul instructs slaves to be obedient to their masters with sincerity and as to Christ (6:5). In Paul's day, slavery was rampant. A very high percentage of the Roman world were slaves. This work force consisted not only of domestic servants and manual laborers, but also of highly educated people. Masters considered slaves chattels and living tools whom they could treat in any manner they wished.

Paul's mention of slaves indicates that the church included slaves. Paul exhorts them to serve their masters as if they are serving the Lord. In fact, he stresses this fact by mentioning Christ in verses 5, 6, 7, and 8. Christ has liberated the slave; the slave, therefore, performs his earthly tasks as part of following God's will. No longer does the slave perform well only when the eyes of the master are looking at him (6:6). Twentieth-century employees are no different. They have contracted to serve an employer and, therefore, must give total effort in performing their tasks. They should not be busy only when the boss is looking, but give a 100 percent effort at all times. Why? Because we ultimately serve the Lord. With good will and godly intentions, employees render service as to the Lord and not to men (6:7). They do their work heartily as if working directly for the Lord (Col. 3:23).

The incentive for the slaves in Paul's day and for employees in the modern age is not temporal reward, although such rewards may come. Slaves and employees are encouraged in their service, even if mundane and tedious, by the realization that whatever good they do in the service of others, they will receive blessings back from the Lord (6:8). The greatest reward will come at the judgment seat of Christ when He says, "Well done, good and faithful servant" (Matt. 25:21). We as members of Christ's body must remember that in our everyday work-world and in our service to others the Lord has not called us to be successful, but to be faithful. Our work efforts should be fueled by our desire to labor for the Lord and not by our desire to earn money or fame.

Masters and Employers (6:9)

Paul did not cease with instructing slaves. The Christian community also included masters like Philemon, who served the one true master, the Lord Jesus Christ. Both the slave and the master were ultimately responsible to Christ, and "there is no partiality with Him" (6:9). Paul exhorts the masters to treat their slaves fairly and "give up threatening" them (6:9). They should treat them in the same way they expect to be served. If masters want respect from their slaves, they must treat them with respect. If they want good and faithful service, they must serve their slaves by providing for them, protecting them, and treating them as members of their households.

Likewise, modern employers must treat their employees with respect by giving them a fair wage and providing a good working environment. They should not threaten, badger, or browbeat their employees, but rather display an attitude of care and concern. They serve them by managing with the employees' best interests in mind. Godly employers realize that they serve Jesus Christ, who is not a respecter of persons, for there is no partiality with God between an employer and his employees.

Did Paul Support Slavery?

Some commentators believe Paul supported slavery because he did not forthrightly condemn it. Rather, he instructed both slaves and masters, which seems to give his seal of approval on the institution. For some critics, this is an inadequate response. They believe Paul should have instructed Christian masters to emancipate their slaves.

Although Paul gives no command to masters to free their slaves, he does emphasize the brotherhood of man. In fact, brotherhood is a major theme in Paul's letter to the Ephesians, for he teaches that God's new society consists of God's household, which comprises all kinds of people who become related to each other as brothers and sisters in Christ. In his letter to the Galatians Paul strongly states that there is neither bond nor free in Christ Jesus, but all are one under the Lord's headship (Gal. 3:28).

Slavery was a critical ingredient for the survival of the Roman economy. The Roman government also took steps to protect slaves and provide freedom in certain situations. In fact, history records the emancipation of great numbers of slaves in the first century B.C. For Paul to incite slaves to rebellion would be a sin against God and to hinder the present movement of fair treatment to slaves. Furthermore, it would confirm the suspicion of those who sought to destroy Christianity that the apostles preached the gospel in order to subvert and destroy Roman society.

Paul, therefore, took the diplomatic approach and stated the principles of the gospel in such a manner that he left the decision of emancipating a slave to the conscience of the master. The Letter to Philemon is a perfect example of Paul's approach. Though he didn't instruct Philemon to release Onesimus, Paul hinted broadly that this is what he expected Philemon to do. "And I have sent him back to you in person, that is, sending my very heart, whom I wished to keep with me" (Philem. 12-13). Paul advised Philemon that Onesimus is no longer a slave, but rather a beloved brother (Philem. 16) in his service. Paul preached the gospel (including that there is no slave in Christ) and then left the words to act upon Philemon's conscience. He did not obligate Philemon to emancipate Onesimus.

The choice was Philemon's as he responded to the gospel (Philem. 14). Paul accomplished his purpose in a way that did not fuel the fires of his enemies.

Application of Ephesians 6:1-9

1. As a parent I will show my children love, honor, and respect for my spouse by _____
_____ (doing something in front of the children).

   Applied: Yes _____   No _____

2. I will instruct my children in the ways of the Lord by praying with them for _____ minutes per day.

   Applied: Yes _____   No _____

3. *Parents:* I will spend at least one intimate and special hour this week with each of my children.

   Applied: Yes _____   No _____

   Singles without children: I will ask _____
   _____ (name of child) to _____
   (special activity) and endeavor to show him or her the love of Christ in my life.

   Applied: Yes _____   No _____

4. I will do something special for _____
_____ (co-worker or friend) by _____
_____ (the action).

   Applied: Yes _____   No _____

Questions for Ephesians 6:10-24

1. Whom does Paul say our real struggles are with (6:12)? Paul calls us to battle. Do you feel stimulated by the call (6:13)? Why or why not?

   a.

   b. Yes _____ No _____.

2. What are the five main defensive pieces of armor God has given
   us (6:14-17)? How is each one rooted in Christ? Notice that not
   one piece goes on our back. What does this suggest?

   a.

   b.

   c.

3. What major weapon has God given us to fight the battle (6:17)?
   What does Hebrews 4:12 say about this weapon? In what three
   ways did Jesus use this weapon in His wilderness testing (Matt.
   4:1-11)?

   a.

b.

c. (1)

(2)

(3)

13

Spiritual Warfare

────────── *6:10-24* ──────────

Principalities and Powers (6:10-12)

Paul first encourages the believers to be submissive to one another (5:21) and then to establish strong biblical relationships between husbands and wives (5:22-33), parents and children (6:1-4), and masters and slaves (6:5-9). Part of the reason for having a biblical relationship is to be prepared for the battle ahead. "Be strong in the Lord, and in the strength of His might," says Paul (6:10). Strength in the Lord is the essential ingredient for fighting against the "schemes of the devil" (6:11). An individual cannot war against the principalities and powers in his own might, for he does not stand a chance. He can, however, do all things through Christ, who strengthens him (Phil. 4:13). Christ imparts His power to the community of faith. As members of His body, believers must act as one fighting unit in order to consistently frustrate the strategy of Satan.

Paul was well aware of the strategies of Satan. He wrote of the obstacles Satan placed in the path of his apostolic ministry (I Thess. 2:18). He warned husbands and wives about the temptations Satan would use to ruin an intimate relationship (I Cor. 7:5). He counseled believers to be aware of Satan's craftiness. Though Satan may appear as an angel of light, he teaches falsely and leads people away from devotion to Christ (II Cor. 11:3). The believer must call on God's strength to expose and do battle against the devices and tactics of Satan. The real battle takes place not on the human plane, "but against the powers, against the world forces of this darkness, and against the spiritual forces of wickedness in the heavenly places" (6:12).

Paul mentioned principalities and powers earlier in this letter in a general sense (1:21; 3:10). They are the highest angel-princes who, although created by Christ (Col. 1:16), rebelled against Him and sought worship and homage by men. Believers must remember that Christ wrestled with these rebels, overcame them, and disarmed them (Col. 2:15). Although Christ has vanquished these evil powers, He allows them to roam about and harass even Christians, for God uses the harassment of trials and tribulations to perfect a believer toward maturity in Christ (James 1:4). As foes, these powers have already been defeated, but individual battles remain. A Christian must learn how to put on God's armor for protection and for waging war.

The Armor of God (6:13-17)

Paul previously warned his readers to walk carefully as wise men because the days are evil (5:15-16). He now sounds reveille and tells his readers to "take up the full armor of God" in order "to resist in the evil day" by standing firm (6:13). How does one stand firm? By learning how to wear the armor and enter the battle with God's protection. Christians should be warriors, not wimps. Without a firm foothold in Christ, Christians become an easy target for the devil. Paul emphasizes Christian stability as a prerequisite for withstanding the onslaught of the enemy.

"The full armor of God" is translated from the Greek word *panoplia*. It connotes the complete armor worn by a heavily armed Roman soldier. Paul wants his readers to understand the necessity of wearing God's divine protection. Otherwise, the devil will subdue them by his wiles. God as our general wants us to partake of the spiritual battles, for persevering through them molds our characters and aids us in becoming more Christ-like. We must not be "pew sitters," but rather trench fighters. We must go to war against the forces of evil. "Attack" is the battle cry, and the gates of hell will not prevail (Matt. 16:18).

What is the armor God gives us? First is the girdle or belt of truth (6:14). A Roman soldier's belt was made of leather and was used to gather his tunic together and to secure his sword. To tighten one's belt meant to prepare for the battle ahead. The Christian warrior's belt is truth, which includes honesty, sincerity, loyalty, and faithfulness in everyday life. But to whom does the believer direct this truth? To the one who is the Truth, that is, Jesus Christ (John 14:6). Jesus is our objective Truth while honesty, sincerity, loyalty, and faithfulness are the subjective truths by which we live.

Second is the breastplate of righteousness (6:14). Although a soldier's breastplate often covered his back, some did not. They were worn to cover the chest and were secured in the back. Paul may have also pictured the breastpiece of judgment worn by the high priests (Exod. 28:15-30). On this breastpiece were enscrolled the twelve tribes of Israel whom the high priest represented to God. The high priest was the proxy of righteousness in character and conduct for all the tribes, for no unrighteous person would dare approach a holy and righteous God. A Christian soldier's breastplate also stood for a righteous lifestyle, which would resist the temptations of the devil. Yet, his lifestyle would have no meaning or value unless he was first justified through Christ, who clothes us with His righteousness (I Cor. 1:30; Isa. 61:10; Rom. 4:11).

Third are the gospel boots. "Shod your feet with the preparation of the gospel of peace" (6:15). The Roman boot that Paul probably had in mind was the *caliga* ("half-boot"). The half-boot was a partial sandal with the toes exposed. It was made of leather with straps to tie it to the ankles and shins. The sole was heavily studded to prevent slippage as the wearer stood in battle. The Christian soldier's boots are the gospel of peace. He should be prepared, ready, and firm to present the gospel, to make a defense, and to give an account of the hope that is within him (I Pet. 3:15). Every believer bears good news that publishes peace (Isa. 52:7). What is that good news? That Jesus gave His life as God's peacemaker (2:14) to reconcile His elect to Himself (2:15). Satan fears and hates those who carry the gospel of peace, because through it God rescues people from the tyranny of Satan's enslavement.

Fourth is the shield of faith, which a Christian uses to ward off the flaming darts of the evil one (2:16). The shield (*thureos*) is not the small round one used by the Greeks, but the large oblong one commonly used by the Romans, which protected from the neck to the feet. It was made of wood, covered with linen and hide, and bound with iron. It not only stopped the thrust of a missile, but also put out the fiery darts and arrows projected at the soldier. The darts of the devil can be all sorts of temptations, accusations, guilt, and thoughts that inflame our consciences to disobey or rebel against God. God in His wisdom has given us the shield of faith, which can stop the thrust of the flaming missiles and even put out the fire. God Himself is "a shield to those who take refuge in Him" (Prov. 30:5). Our refuge is Jesus Christ, for without faith in Him we have no protection from the incendiary attacks of the devil.

Fifth is the "helmet of salvation" (6:17). The helmet of a Roman soldier was made of bronze, iron, or some other tough metal. Some of the helmets were also decorated with plumes or crests. The Christian's helmet is his adornment, for the hope of his salvation (I Thess. 5:8) is a confident expectation of resurrection glory with the Lord. Assurance of salvation enables a Christian warrior to enter the battle with the knowledge that victory has already been gained in Christ, "for he who has the Son has life" (I John 5:12). Salvation is in Christ alone (John 14:6). Therefore, when we put on our helmets, we acknowledge our salvation in Christ.

The Offensive Weapon (6:17).

The only weapon God gives the Christian warrior is "the sword of the Spirit which is the Word of God" (6:17). Paul uses the Greek word *rhēma*, the spoken Word of God. God's Word (*logos*) is "living and active and sharper than any two-edged sword" (Heb. 4:12). Yet, if we leave the written Word, the Bible, unused on a nightstand or mutilate it by misinterpretation, it becomes a sword dulled by inactivity or broken from misuse. We must speak and apply its truths. The Israelites trembled at God's spoken word, for He executed judgment on a disobedient people by slaying them with the words of His mouth (Hos. 6:5). A sharp sword proceeding from the mouth of the coming Messiah will smite the nations (Rev. 19:15).

The Bible is God's revealed weapon, given to His church to cut away man's defenses and penetrate into his heart, causing death to the old man but giving life to the new (II Cor. 5:17). For a believer, the sword of the Spirit becomes a parrying weapon to resist temptations from the devil. Jesus used the Scriptures in three ways to counter the devil's attack in the wilderness. First, using it as a manual for life, Jesus said, "It is written, man shall not live on bread alone, but on every word that proceeds out of the mouth of God" (Matt. 4:4). As the Israelites existed on manna, the believer exists on the breath of God, His inspired Word. The Scripture is our road map for life, a manual that provides our needs and tells us how to live.

Second, Jesus used the Scriptures as a defensive weapon against Satan's challenge to throw Himself from the pinnacle of the temple. Satan used Scripture out of context and twisted God's words. Jesus parried the devil's attack, saying, "On the other hand, it is written, 'You shall not tempt the Lord your God'" (Matt. 4:7). Jesus used God's Word to support His stance.

Third, Jesus used God's Word as an offensive weapon. In refusing Satan's offer of kingdoms and glory, Jesus employed the Scriptures to counterattack the devil. "Begone, Satan! For it is written, 'You shall worship the Lord your God and serve Him only'" (Matt. 4:10). Jesus took the offensive and struck forth with God's two-edged sword. As fellow heirs with Christ, we also have the ability to use God's Word to launch an attack against our enemy, the serpent.

As Christians, we must learn to fight not with our own wisdom, but with God's Word. If we never unsheath the Bible, we will find ourselves in battle without a weapon, dodging darts. However, not only must we arm ourselves with God's Word, Jesus Christ (John 1:1, 14), but we must also put on the complete armor, summed up in Jesus Christ. Lacking one piece leaves us vulnerable and uncovered. Putting on the armor and then turning from the conflict leaves our backsides exposed. We must face the conflicts and stand firm against the enemy, for if we resist him, he will flee (James 4:7). Resistance should be corporate; Paul is speaking to groups of believers. Soldiers fighting together win wars; an individual who takes on a superior force is foolish.

Many believers are worthless warriors. They tremble and run at the first sign of problems. They seek to avoid conflict and controversy under the guise of unity and peace. Yet, Christ said He did not come to bring peace to the world but a sword (Matt. 10:34). Believers are drafted into the army of Christ. Too many "Christians" have gone AWOL (absent without leave). Those who refuse to fight and to face painful situations commit mutiny.

A Support Weapon (6:18-20)

Once armed, the believer receives auxiliary support in prayer. "With all prayer and petition pray at all times in the Spirit," says Paul (6:18). As artillery supports the infantry, prayer supports the wielding of the sword of the Spirit. Prayer should not be used only occasionally, but at all times, for it goes hand in hand with the word of God. Prayer must be prompted and guided by the Holy Spirit and not be mere "puffs of smoke." We must earnestly seek the Lord's face.

By praying diligently, a believer will be alert as a good soldier "with all perseverance" (6:18). Satan is the great deceiver. If a Christian is not watchful, deceptive teaching or worldly conformity may subtly overtake him. A soldier also relies on his buddy to protect his rear or flank. So, too, a Christian must watch over other believers.

Paul asks others to watch over him; he requests their prayers (6:19) to strengthen him in furthering the claims of the gospel. He was Christ's ambassador in chains (6:20), waging war from prison. He needed encouragement to continue speaking boldly the mystery of Christ. He did so for two more years while under house arrest (Acts 28:30-31).

Conclusion (6:21-24)

Paul concludes his letter with final greetings. He probably dictated his letter to Tychicus, whom he calls a beloved brother who would relate everything to his readers (6:21). Tychicus probably carried the letter to Ephesus. He would tell the recipients about Paul and comfort them concerning their Roman brothers (6:22).

Paul ends his letter in the traditional style of proclaiming a wish. First, he wishes for peace to the brethren and love with faith (6:23). Peace and love should be inseparable, for peace brings reconciliation (between Jew and Gentile, men and God), but love is the source of peace. Love should also emanate from the reconciliation and be seen through the exercise of faith.

Second, Paul wishes that "grace be with all those who love" the Lord (6:24). This love is incorruptible or unfailing. Paul opened his letter with greetings of grace and peace (1:2). He now closes with a similar expression, for it was the atoning work of Jesus Christ that brought peace through reconciliation with God. This peace was accomplished only by God's grace. Paul prays that God's new society (Jew and Gentile together) will experience this peace by living in harmony with one another.

Application of Ephesians 6:10-24

1. I realize I am in spiritual battle and need the constant support of other believers. I will _____/will not _____ (check one) endeavor to build my relationships with others. I choose _____/ choose not _____ (check one) to be accountable to other believers.

2. There is a need in my life for more study and application of God's word. Yes _____ No _____. I, therfore, propose to _____
_____
_____ (do something).